FIGHTING FOR FREEDOM

7 Battles Women Encounter and the Strategy that Changes Everything

Danielle M. Wingate

ISBN:

978-1-7370575-0-5 paperback
978-1-7370575-1-2 e-book

You, my brothers and sisters, were called to be free. But do not use your freedom to indulge the flesh; rather, serve one another humbly in love.
Galatians 5:13 NIV

Free people free people. We have been given this gift to bring freedom through Jesus to everyone.

Dedication

To my husband and forever teammate, Chris, you are an answered prayer to my life. I am beyond grateful for how you have led and sharpened me. Thank you for fighting for me and our family as you do. You have championed me to know and trust the Father more, and I am undone with gratitude at the life we get to share with our little world changers!

Emmaus, Caleb, Moriah, and Judah—you four are the greatest gifts He has ever entrusted to me. God wastes nothing, and now I can see how every battle has been an opportunity to refine and prepare me to walk alongside you four, championing you and helping you to know the massive call that God has placed on your lives. There are no words to express my deep love, gratitude, and humility for God choosing me to be your mom! I'm beyond proud of who you are and who you are becoming! May you always know the journey is worth it, victory belongs to the Lord, and His ways are always better!

To my Catalyst Women family, I am moved beyond words at what God has done and continues to do through this journey and these relationships. Thank you for your prayers, for being my greatest cheerleaders in the process, and for stepping up to the fight for freedom. Your stories of victory and breakthrough have only inspired me to dig deeper and fight harder for this resource you are holding!

Acknowledgements

This project has been a labor of love and has not been without spiritual warfare through every chapter, but there's no way it would have been what it is without the prayer, love, and support of so many.

Renee Crawford, thank you for your amazing editorial services. You have been an incredible voice of guidance, digging deeper to make this what it is.

Yolanda Conrad, Celeste Gonzalez, Mikella VanDyke, Polly Payne, Morgan Campey, and Kacy Kincaid, thank you for reading through the early stages of the book, giving guidance, prayer, and support! You helped push me forward in countless ways!

Stephanie Hodges and TJ Fletcher, thank you for lighting the writing spark under me again to get back to what I had started. We are far better with community and accountability, and you both have been that for me!

Priscilla Shirer, I know Jesus personally as my Lord and Savior because of your obedience and deep love for Him. Thank you for following His call. Thank you for being the catalyst to awaken my heart and soul to Him.

Jenny Donnelly, Heather Schott, Lori Champion, Lisa Bevere, Emily Cummins, Renee Christiensen, Celeste and Daniel Gonzalex, Allie Gorman, Candace Oliver, Sandy Van Alstine, Janell King, Daphne Zuniga, Tammey Stokely, Danielle Torrez, Kristen Pannell, Constance Karwandyar, Brittany Roth, Lorrie Loeffler, Bruce Loeffler, Jim and Sue Ann Wingate, Mike Vest, Kevin Cook, Brian Dishon, Blake Bergstrom, Stephen and Jackie Brewster—each of you have been instrumental in this journey, and I am deeply thankful for the friendship, leadership, guidance, and prayers!

Table of Contents

Introduction

Life is filled with moments of impact, *catalyst* experiences. Encounters and conversations that shift our perspective, causing us to pause, to respond, and, ultimately experiences that leave a lasting impression. In 2015, the movie *War Room* was one of those key "moments of impact" for me. I was living many answered prayers from the Lord—enjoying my first year of marriage and being newly pregnant with our first daughter. I always desired to be married; however, my world was rocked. There I was, a new wife, a new military spouse, and a mother to be, plus we had moved from my home in Nashville, TN to Belton, TX to be stationed at Fort Hood. My pretty, picture-perfect life together—community, attending my church together, family nearby, etc. was different. Everything was new, nothing was familiar. While I probably should have felt happiness and excitement at the adventure, I struggled with deep loneliness, sadness, fear, loss of purpose, and even resentment towards my husband.

To give context to the movie, Elizabeth Jordan, a realtor (played by Priscilla Shirer), is experiencing a rough season with her husband. He is headed towards an affair. He travels constantly for work, and the family dynamic is crumbling. One day, she meets a new client, Ms. Clara, an elderly widow who is well-experienced in the "battlefield" of marriage. Ms. Clara builds a relationship with Elizabeth and mentors her in the importance of fighting for her husband and not with him. She teaches Elizabeth to view her husband in a different light—not as the enemy. Ms. Clara comes alongside Elizabeth during this season to help equip her with the right tools for the right warfare.

The movie opens with a strategic planning meeting with military officials in a war zone. The correlation? There is a war taking place all day, every day, all around us. Each day not only is our marriage on the battlefield, but every other aspect of our lives.

We have an enemy: Satan, the fallen angel, and the archenemy of God, is out to steal, kill, and destroy you and me. This means he is operating in the supernatural realm—contemplating with his demons, studying us, and planning against us. Why? Satan is determined to rule the whole Earth, and to destroy us in the process. He intends to steal our joy, kill any intimacy with God, and destroy any opportunity to make us see or believe that God has designed us and called us for a purpose. Our enemy is often referred to as the father of lies; Satan replaces truth with lies and gives subtle misdirection to make us doubt God's faithfulness. He will make us doubt pieces of God's Word, and, ultimately, question God's plan for our lives.

So it is in the conflict between Satan and the believer, God's child can conquer everything by prayer. Is it any wonder that Satan does his utmost to snatch that weapon from the Christian, or to hinder him in the use of it?

—Andrew Murray, *The Prayer Life*

With nothing to lose, Elizabeth heeds Ms. Clara's guidance. She cleans out her closet, making it her "war room" where she goes to battle, fighting the war raging against her marriage, her husband, and her family through prayer and surrender. In the end, she witnesses a godly transformation in her marriage. Her husband is impacted through her actions and obedience to Christ, her tenacity to go after the right fight. Everything changes.

What Would You Do?

If you knew that someone was intentionally plotting against someone you loved to make their life more stressful, what would you do? If an attacker was tormenting someone you loved with pressures of the world, trying to make them crumble, feeding the lie that life would be better without them, what would you do?

It's happening—to me, to you, and to every aspect of our lives. Any place where Satan and his demons can find entry points, to access inside, they will. It's not only your life that the enemy wants to wreck, but every...single...person's life. Satan may use you, your spouse, someone else, or even your own kids to deceive and distract you. Think about it, as I write this, there are about 7.5 billion people in our world. As mentioned in Luke 22:31, if each person isn't on guard against the real enemy, they will find themselves living life in limiting and frustrating ways that God never intended for them to. You may be showing up every day to your life, your marriage, your family, your workplace, and the circles in which you do life, fighting the wrong enemy.

We assign blame. We judge. We become bitter. We confront people and circumstances thinking "they are the problem" or "this thing is the problem" when really, they aren't. They may be a decoy, totally unaware that they are being used to distract us, and steal what God has for us in this season.

The person or thing that you think is your enemy isn't the real enemy.

Welcome to the war.

In this book, I will help you suit up with the right "armor" and create strategies to fight the real enemy and win the battles as they arise. Will it be easy? No. Will it mean that your marriage will be challenge free? No. Will it mean that you will have less challenges? Probably not… let's be honest, we are human.

However, through a new perspective, a new approach, and a new fight against the real enemy, you will experience greater hope, confidence, and assurance as you engage your battles. Suiting up with the right armor will set the example for your kids and their future families and give you strength beyond your human ability to know that you are addressing the root issue and not simply the symptoms.

Ready?

Here are some things you will find in *Fighting for Freedom* to help you along the way as you prepare for battle.

1. The first three chapters are foundation pieces to the battle.
2. At the end of each battle chapter, there is a four-step example to help you identify lies of the enemy and replace them with God-given truths.
3. Following the battle strategy, I have shared a fighting tip. This is a single practical element taught in martial arts, providing insight into the basics of self-defense.
4. Prayer. I have written a prayer not only for me, but for you as well. Pray this, or something similar, and believe that your Heavenly Father hears it, and loves you, and is at work for you!
5. Discussion questions are a great tool to dig deeper for application. Maybe you are reading this by yourself, with one friend, or ten; these questions are intended to be a guide to generate authentic dialogue and promote accountability for change.

There are seven theme-based battles, each reviewing a key area that you will encounter, along with examples of lies the enemy whispers and key scriptures to help you build out your own battle plan for victory. In the back of the book, there are a few additional keys to true freedom: fasting, tithing, and sabbathing.

Seven Battles

Battle 1: Your Heart
Battle 2: Your Mind
Battle 3: Your Words
Battle 4: Your Past
Battle 5: Your Present
Battle 6: Your Future
Battle 7: Your Calling

My prayer is that you will begin to identify and recognize the attacks in your own life, and then formulate your own personal battle strategy against the lies and tactics as they arise.

I may not be sitting across from you at coffee, and we may never physically meet, but I am praying for you, believing that this book is going to be an encouragement and tool as you grow in your freedom in Jesus!

You need to know this, because the enemy is going to tell you things contradictory to the truth of God. Slight variations that sound like the truth, or that seem to make sense, but they aren't from God. Be encouraged, picking up this book is a great step in the right direction. I'm excited for the journey ahead! Hurt people hurt people, but free people free other people. Freedom belongs to you, sister! You are a daughter of the King, fully known, fully loved, and widely celebrated for who you are today, and who you are becoming! You are worth it all to Him, and He has great plans for your life. I pray something inside of you rises, eager to fight the right fight.

I have told you these things, so that in me you may have peace. In this world you will have trouble. But take heart! I have overcome the world.
—John 16:33 NIV

1
The Enemy + The War

The thief comes only to steal and kill and destroy; I have come that they may have life, and have it to the full.— John 10:10 NIV

One night in a dream, I found myself in an open field. A short distance away, countless women were doubled over. Each woman had a toylike windup piece in her back. Bent over, these women had been crushed from the weight of the world. Overpowered by expectations, opinions, unmet needs, desires, and sadness from shame. Feeling unworthy, unwanted, and unqualified, like failures. Sadness from regret, from bitterness, and from loss of purpose had taken its toll. To my surprise, not one woman seemed bothered or alarmed by this posture or identity. This doubled-over and overburdened posture had actually become normal. Worse, this was what the women believed they deserved. Tears filled my eyes as I stood realizing the enemy had deceived each of them.

The Enemy

To understand the war, we need to know who our enemy is and why he hates us. The thief that John refers to goes by many names: Satan, Lucifer, Devil, Tempter, Ruler of the World, Prince of Darkness, Accuser, and Father of Lies. Satan was an angel in Heaven first, but he desired to be above God.

> *How you have fallen from heaven, O Lucifer, son of the morning! . . . For you have said in your heart: "I will ascend into heaven, I will exalt my throne above the stars of God; I will also sit on the mount of the congregation on the farthest sides of the north; I will ascend above the heights of the clouds, I will be like the Most High."*— Isaiah 14:12-14 NKJV

> *You had the seal of perfection, full of wisdom and perfect in beauty.... You were the anointed cherub who covers, and I placed you there. You were on the holy mountain of God; you walked in the midst of the stones of fire. You were blameless in your ways from the day you were created until unrighteousness was found in you. By the abundance of your trade you were internally filled with violence, and you sinned; therefore I have cast you as profane from the mountain of God.... Your heart was lifted up because of your beauty; you corrupted your wisdom by reason of your splendor. I cast you to the ground.* — Ezekiel 28:12, 14-17 NASB

We were created from God and in His image. Out of His deep love for us, God positioned humans higher than the angels, giving us free-will for relationships and eternity. Out of jealousy for God's position and hate for humanity, Satan and other angels chose to rebel. Satan has been given temporary authority to rule on Earth, but one day he and his demons will be sentenced to Hell for eternity. Until that time, he and his dark angels are out to steal, kill, and keep us from finding a relationship with the Father and prevent others from knowing Jesus Christ.

Then He will also say to those on His left, "Depart from Me, accursed ones, into the eternal fire which has been prepared for the devil and his angels;"
—Matthew 25:41 NASB

Hollywood has created the figure of Satan to be some mischievous little red guy with horns and a tail, running around causing havoc. Hollywood missed the accuracy of his image. Satan used to be an angel, and one of the highest. According to Ezekiel 28, he was the seal of perfection, so he's probably beautiful. Second Corinthians 11:14-15 (NLT) says, *"Even Satan disguises himself as an angel of light. It is no wonder that his servants also disguise themselves as servants of righteousness."* **The key here is deception —this is how Satan operates.** From the beginning, he has created scenarios, conversations, and events to distract us. He implements misleading encounters where we question the goodness of God, while stirring up competition, jealousy, pride, and hate. Often, sin is packaged attractively, usually disguised as something that seems similar to what is deeply desired. At first look, the thing or action appears good, sounds right, or feels innocent. In the light, we see it for what it really is, a counterfeit.

Our enemy's tactics haven't changed. When we aren't spending time with the Father daily and in His Word, we unintentionally leave ourselves open for attacks. Here's an example: a thought enters our mind. No problem with that, right? Over time, our enemy and strategy fades into the background as someone or something that we associate with innocence and familiarity. "That thing? Oh, yeah, that has been there for months." We let down our guard. We don't see anything wrong or suspicious. Until one day, Satan casually introduces someone or something, most likely harmless. Over time, and a message comes through reinforcing that thought. Casually our mind begins to process how this all seems innocent, harmless, and like a normal encounter that could happen to anyone. Our enemy continues to invade. Slowly, subtly, and deceptively, Satan introduces little things that look good, feel right, and seem close to the truth. He operates with both great patience and intentionality.

If he can get us to buy into the lie, ignore God's Word, and lower our guard, unknowingly we have given permission to our enemy to reside. Our enemy sets no limits for himself on how far he will go. With undetected access, he targets our self-image, our beliefs, our family, our dreams, our fears, and anything that we love.

No one is free from the attacks of the enemy, but not all fall victim to it. God has ultimate authority. Romans 8:31 (NIV) says, "*What then shall we say to these things? If God is for us, who can be against us?*" It's up to us to decide who we turn to. The choice is ours as to whose truth we believe and whom we live for. Our purpose remains the same—to spread the Word of Christ so that more may know Jesus and be reunited with their Heavenly Father.

For our struggle is not against flesh and blood, but against the rulers, against the powers, against the world forces of this darkness, against the spiritual forces of wickedness in the heavenly places.— Ephesians 6:12 NASB

When you hear the term "enemy", what comes to mind? These days it can feel like the enemy is easily conceptualized with whoever and whatever the media is telling us is the problem. Or maybe your enemy feels like someone you know. While those are valid, John is talking about a certain enemy. The king of enemies. A person, being, or force that is a greater threat beyond comprehension.

We need to know about this enemy and aware of his strategies, but not to be afraid of him. There is more happening around us than what we realize. Satan would love for us to be isolated with a loss of purpose, a loss of vision, a loss of self-worth, and a loss of passion. **If Satan can make us believe a lie, unintentionally, we have allowed his tactics of deception and the toxic symptoms that come with it to take root in our lives.** We must take back the authority God has given us.

The War

We are in a war because of pride and rebellion. Satan first rebelled against God. Satan deceived Eve and Adam into eating the forbidden fruit. Battles always began internally, then manifest physically. As opposition rises spiritually to blind and harden the hearts of people, we are activated as believers. Psalm 89:14 (NIV) states, "*Righteousness and justice are the foundation of [God's] throne; love and faithfulness go before [God].*" God does not and cannot contradict Himself. **The presence of unrighteousness and injustice is the physical manifestation of spiritual warfare.** The Lord has won the battle, but He still calls us to fight at times. As sons and daughters, He has chosen us to spread the word of His Son, to proclaim freedom and truth. In every battle, He faithfully provides a strategy to carry out His will. He is sovereign. He holds the ultimate power. Scripture is filled with battles and strategies, victorious in both obedience and submission.

The Lord Is with You

Jehoshaphat was the king of Judah. He loved the Lord, led justly and humbly, and brought glory and honor to God. He heard of a coming invasion. "Jehoshophat *was afraid and turned his attention to seek the LORD, and proclaimed a fast throughout all Judah. So Judah gathered together to seek help from the LORD; they even came from all the cities of Judah to seek the LORD"* (2 Chronicles 20:3-4 NASB). Then, Jehoshaphat petitioned the Lord, "*Should evil come upon us, the sword, or judgment, or pestilence, or famine, we will stand before this house and before You...and cry to You in distress, and You will hear and deliver us.... nor do we know what to do, but our eyes are on You"* (2 Chronicles 20:9, 12 NASB). The Lord answered his prayer. The Holy Spirit gave Jahaziel, a man in the assembly, a word of victory. "*Do not fear or be dismayed because of this great multitude, for the battle is not yours but God's.... You need not fight in this battle; station yourselves, stand and see the salvation of the LORD on your behalf.... Do not fear or be dismayed; tomorrow go out to face them, for the LORD is with you"* (2 Chronicles 20:15, 17 NASB). They all fell down and worshipped God. The next morning, they rose and did as the Lord instructed. Jehoshaphat sent out the worship leaders ahead of the army. "*When they began singing and praising, the LORD set ambushes against [those] who had come against Judah"* (2 Chronicles 20:22 NASB). The enemies were destroyed before Judah even came to the lookout point.

Fear was the attack against King Jehoshaphat. God doesn't give fear. So, who did? Satan. A physical war was coming, an attack far greater than what Judah could succeed against. The king didn't wait for the physical battle; he took it to the Lord first. He presented the feeling of fear before the Lord to get both his heart and mind ready for what the Lord had for Judah.

The Word is filled with faithful plans and promises from God:

- Exodus 14—Pharaoh pursued the Israelites; God parted the sea as Moses stepped into the water.
- Joshua 6—Israel marched around the city of Jericho seven times, and the walls fell down.

- Joshua 10—Five kings of the Amorites set an ambush; the Lord sent a hailstorm, which killed more men than the actual battle did.
- Judges 7- 8—Gideon took three hundred soldiers to battle against thousands of Midianites.
- 1 Samuel 17—David killed Goliath by trusting in God and picking up a rock.

Our battle belongs to God, but we still fight. Our fight should always begin with prayer and worship, walking in obedience, submission, and sometimes more. We first position our hearts and minds for whatever He asks so that we are ready. One day we will be reunited with Him. Until then, we are on a mission, called as believers to go out, wherever we are to spread the word of Jesus. God has won the war.

Mission Ready

As an Army wife, I have a second-row seat to war. My amazing husband is an aviation officer in the US Army. I say "second-row," because I have physically never been to enemy lines. I have never encountered someone wanting to kill me or someone who hates my very existence. As I write this, my husband has served for eighteen years. He has been deployed to war zones collectively for forty-nine months—four years of his life. We have walked through four of these deployments together. None of them easy, with every mission and strategy different from the last.

Chis is always training. Leadership is always strategizing with great foresight, knowing an enemy can arise at a moment's notice. His unit's response to protect and defend is never a question of if, but when opposition rises. My husband, along with other soldiers find gratitude and fulfillment in deploying and going down range. It is what they have trained for. Every day, every week, and for eighteen years, my husband has been stretched and conditioned to fight an enemy. Monthly Chris sends a report to the Brigade's leadership notating the level of "readiness," meaning if the call to deploy came today, how soon would the team be ready to go?

There are regular exercises and training events that require great work, in-depth planning, and long hours. If I'm not mindful, the purpose and strategy behind the training escapes me. I focus on what is before me—long days with the kids, seasons of pseudo-single parenting, additional stress, and minimal time and communication from my husband.

Isn't this also true in our spiritual lives? We should be training, conditioning our hearts and our minds for battle. Daily, we should be worshipping, coming before the Lord for our daily strategy to bring us close to the heart of our Father, as He preps us for His victory. It's easy to miss it. It's easy to focus on just another day, another busy season, another year of whatever feels mundane, long, and repetitive. But what if this is where He has positioned us to train? What if this very season is when we are to stretch and condition, as we exercise and prepare for what He has in store for us?

Victory Belongs to the Lord

Come back to the dream with me for a moment. Fervently, I went to one woman and began turning the metal toylike key in her back. Each turn met with resistance, but her posture was changing. My doubled-over sister began to straighten and stand tall. Vibrant color filled her face, her eyes sparkled, and a genuine smile emerged. Fog cleared from around her, scale-like items fell from her eyes, as a sense of joy came forth. She realized that she had been in bondage to the lies of the enemy. With haste, we both ran to fellow women and began turning the keys in their backs. Woman after woman began to awaken, each coming back to life and realizing their value and truth.

After I woke up, I prayed, "God, is this what women are battling internally? **Are we so isolated and inundated with everything that we are missing what you have created us for?"** He impressed on my heart that this was never His intent for us. Rather, He has designed us to live free and whole in His presence and love. Not just so we can live our best lives, but free so that our lives would reflect Him to the world and lead others to freedom. Then I found Luke 13:11-12 (NASB): "*And there was a woman who for* *eighteen years had had a sickness caused by a spirit; and she was bent double, and could not straighten up at all. When Jesus saw her, He called her over and said to her, 'Woman, you are freed from your sickness.' And He laid His hands on her; and immediately she was made erect again and began glorifying God."*

We are to reflect His grace, His mercy, His love, and His truth, impacting everyone around us with the message of Jesus. This is your God, your Father. He is the One who gave His Son for you; the One who healed the woman plagued by a sickness for twelve years; the One who raised a child from the dead; and the One who exchanged rejection and abandonment for success, provision, and triumph in stories about Joseph, Noah, and Moses. If He did it for them, He will do it for us. This is the foundation we must have as we move forward in faith—God will establish our steps and withhold no good thing from us. This is the posture in which we stand in obedience and submission. He has won the war but asks us to fight so that we may glorify Him and know His will for us in the process.

The question is not if we have trials. The question is when. We are called to be mission-ready, every single day. **Your purpose is too great, your calling is too high, and your legacy is too valuable not to engage in the battle.** You were designed for such a time as this, and it is by no accident that you are here, that your story has been what it has, and that you are walking in this season.

Prayer

Father, thank You that You have won every battle. Thank You for giving Your Living Word so that I can read it and know You better. I trust You. I trust the plans You have for me, and I glorify You for what You are doing in my training. Let the scales fall off, open my eyes. Reveal to me areas where the enemy has residence. In Jesus' name, I rebuke all tactics from the enemy. In Jesus' name, I take back my mind, my heart, and my emotions, and I make them submit to the truth of Your Word. Today, I acknowledge that you have made me for more. Ready my heart and mind for battle. Help me to rest in You, to wait upon You, and to trust You. Thank You for Your grace. Thank You for Your mercy. To God be the glory. Amen.

Discussion Questions

1. Who or what have you identified as your enemy?

2. What do you feel bound by in your life or current season?

3. Where have you unknowingly given permission to the enemy?

4. In what season of your life have you felt like God was preparing you to be "mission-ready"?

2
The Woman + The Warrior

For this reason, rejoice, O heavens and you who dwell in them. Woe to the earth and the sea, because the devil has come down to you with great wrath, knowing that he has only a short time. And when the dragon saw that he was thrown down to the earth, he persecuted the woman who gave birth to the male Child." —Revelation 12:12-13 NASB

The War Against Women

One bright spring afternoon looking out from my screened in porch, I exhaled deeply. I felt numb. As I exhaled, I soaked in the silence with gratitude that I didn't have to put on a mask to perform for anyone. The truth is, I was tired. I felt like I had been running on a track for a long time. It was as if I had been running in circles for years, attempting to carry many things while adding more with each lap around. On the outside I looked happy and successful. It probably seemed like I was doing great, but inside was a different story.

My desire was to portray perfection. I attempted to carry each responsibility with pride and ease while not dropping anything, but I was maxed out. Spiritually, I was out of shape. I wasn't carrying much of anything well. Failure seemed consistent across the board, and worst of all, I felt alone. No one would understand. I wanted off the track, but I felt trapped. Unsure of how to get off or slow down, I tried putting things down, yet equally concerned about what others would think if I stopped or stepped back. Over time, sadness and exhaustion led to regret, confusion, and great frustration. I wanted it to be different. I wanted to feel free. Instead, I worried that if I let people in, or if they knew the real me, I would be rejected and judged. So, I continued to run. I continued to pick up things that seemed valuable and important along the way, while I held up the confident mask.

Years passed. I began asking myself, "What is happening?" Patterns in my life repeated themselves only with different people and places. I began to believe my circumstances were as good as they could get. I began to believe my reality was what I deserved. Growing up in a Christian home, I had heard scripture. I had met believers that lived with a sense of joy, purpose, and freedom. Things I didn't have. Things I wanted. Things I had no idea how to obtain. I would try something new and encounter obstacles. I would try to break free from old patterns and poor choices, but get pulled right back in. I was vulnerable in relationships and got hurt. I had experienced deep hurt by Christian women and ministry leaders. Life felt directionless and on the brink of breaking down. More times than not, I questioned God saying, "Surely this is not all that there is. There has to be more than this."

I have heard the same question from countless women through the years, from a relationship, a financial situation, a medical condition, an unanswered prayer, or an unhealed hurt. **The Bible tells us that we will have trials; the difference is what and whom we give power to in those trials.** Our enemy is always working against us, but he targets women specifically with things like loneliness, fear, image, value, anxiety, self-hate, self-worth, depression, shame, guilt, bitterness, regret, and feeling unqualified. From the beginning God has created a very special calling for women, and our enemy hates it.

Ezer Kenegdo

Be alert and of sober mind. Your enemy the devil prowls around like a roaring lion looking for someone to devour. — 1 Peter 5:8 NIV

Reading this Scripture, I immediately think of Eve. Satan studied her. As a predator, he watched behavior and listened to conversations. Satan approached her when she was in a familiar place and in a way that felt unsuspecting. Her guard was down.

Scripture doesn't tell us why Eve was approached first, but I think Satan saw something extra about her. I wonder if Satan approached Eve first, because he knew that she was a threat to him. Remember, Satan was a high-ranking angel; I imagine he had a close relationship with God. I wonder if Satan knew God's heart, His joy, His pride, and His desire for relationship with man-kind. I wonder if Satan saw the perfect picture of unity, wholeness, and completion when God created Eve after Adam. Maybe Satan heard God speaking to Adam and realized, "This woman is a dangerous weapon, one that must be dealt with immediately."

When God created Eve, the first and most important organization was born— marriage. Marriage is the symbolism that God chose for Christ, the groom, and His bride, the church.

> *Submit to one another out of reverence for Christ. Wives, submit yourselves to your own husbands as you do to the Lord. For the husband is the head of the wife as Christ is the head of the church, his body, of which he is the Savior. Now as the church submits to Christ, so also wives should submit to their husbands in everything. Husbands, love your wives, just as Christ loved the church and gave himself up for her to make her holy, cleansing her by the washing with water through the word, and to present her to himself as a radiant church, without stain or wrinkle or any other blemish, but holy and blameless.* — Ephesians 5:21-27 NIV

It's amazing that marriage, a man, and woman together, portrays the covenant that God establishes with His people. A foreshadowing that His own Son, Jesus would one day sacrifice Himself for us. By laying down His life for us, Jesus' death made us radiant, holy, and blameless so that we could spend eternity in Heaven. **Even on our best days, we would still not be good enough for Heaven if Jesus had not given His life for ours.** I wonder if Satan's jaw dropped.

"The LORD God said, 'It is not good for the man to be alone. I will make a helper suitable for him'" (Genesis 2:18 NASB). In the KJV, the phrase "helper suitable for him" is translated as "help meet". It can also be interpreted as "helpmate", but maybe like me, you have perceived the term as having an inferior or limiting meaning instead of its true intent.

R. David Freedman, former director of the religious studies program at the University of California at Davis, helps unpackage the original meaning of the terms in his article, "Woman. a Power Equal to Man". In Hebrew, the terms "helpmate" and "helpmeet" are derived from two words, *ezer* and *kenegdo. Ezer* has two variations that translates "to rescue, to save" and "to be strong." It is the exact same word that God uses to describe Himself towards humans in eight other verses, and is also a military term to aid in battle:

Blessed are you, Israel!
Who is like you,
a people saved by the LORD?
He is your shield and ***helper***
and your glorious sword.
Your enemies will cower before you,
and you will tread on their heights.
— Deuteronomy 33:29 NIV, emphasis added

The second word, *kenegdo,* is a combination of three different meanings from the Hebrew text. In its truest form, it means "one who stands in front of or opposite to."

God designed women to save, to rescue, to stand on the front lines in opposition, and to face challenges head on in love and truth. Women were created as a solution to complete God's perfect picture of wholeness.

Competition

Have we bought into the lie that women are the weaker, less capable, more inferior sex, or the lie that women need to prove ourselves by overshadowing and silencing men in their roles? Have we begun to believe that to compete, we need to beat men? Is there room for equality? Absolutely!

Should there be fair treatment and pay across the board? 100%! **But what if in our pursuit for more, we have squashed men in the process with our words, our actions, our marketing, and even our beliefs?** Two wrongs don't make a right.

If we look at creation and the infrastructure of marriage, God designed male and female to create wholeness, one complementing and strengthening the other. "Teammates" is the term Chris and I use. God has placed man to be the head of the home, but it doesn't mean that I passively submit or permit anything to happen. We work together. We seek the Lord independently and collectively. We share dialogue. We ask tough questions, and we hold each other accountable. When honest feedback needs to be had, we try and share it in a life-giving way to help better the other.

We are a team. We win together and we lose together. Chris is the best version of himself, when he is running in the lane with the strengths that God has given him. I am the best version of me, when I own and run in my lane in the pursuit of who God has called me to be with my strengths. At times we miss our lanes; he gets in mine, or I in his. Those times are frustrating, confusing, and incredibly unproductive. As a pair of Enneagram threes, unproductivity and delay are infuriating to us! When we run together, in our own lanes, cheering one another on, it is amazing to see how God propels what we are doing and how we grow closer together.

Maybe like me, you have had unfair, offensive, or belittling encounters with a male in the workforce or your community circle. We can't go back and change that. We can't change them, and honestly, remaining mad, hurt, and bitter only hurts us far more in the long run. It doesn't change what happened, and it doesn't protect us from experiencing it again. In a way unlike ever before, men are being attacked, belittled, and silenced. We need them to own their lanes, and us to own ours. The beautiful thing is that the paths are endless, but competing rather than complimenting, and overstepping rather than working together positions us out of alignment with who and what God has designed us to do.

I want to invite you to do something with me, to lead as Jesus would. Leaders go first, and we can lead through change with forgiveness, righteous pursuit, mercy, and confident joy. Even if circumstances haven't changed, an apology hasn't come, or the wound still hurts, we can choose to rise above. Why? Because God is faithful. Because our God is personal, and He knows our story and has a future beyond belief promised for us. His Word is true, and justice belongs to Him. That is our foundation.

Let's not forsake our God-given worth as females for the world's standard. God's way will always be much higher and better and deliver a greater fulfillment than any tangible element the world ever could.

Battle Buddy

For both single and married women, loneliness is a key tactic the enemy uses. Satan wants us to believe that we are the only ones who feel this way and that it will always be this way. One of the best things I have learned while navigating seasons of loneliness and the attacks that come with them is to first find a female who has a relationship with Jesus and second, one whom can be my accountability partner. Military spouses call this person our "battle buddy". A battle buddy provides physical and emotional support for a fellow military spouse during times of deployment. Why? Deployment seasons are often heavily targeted attacks against marriages and families, they are challenging and always a learning curve to navigate. The same can be said in our seasons of greatest attack and vulnerability. We all need other women who stand with us, for us, and help carry us when the attacks are heavy, reminding us of truth. Alone and inward, we leave ourselves vulnerable to limiting beliefs and lies from the enemy.

Moses had people in his corner, that helped him, people who knew his weaknesses, people who supported him when he was tired. The Israelites were in the desert and being attacked by the Amalekites. Joshua was leading the battle, but on a nearby hill stood Moses, Aaron, and Hur. "*So it came about when Moses held his hand up, that Israel prevailed, and when he let his hand down, Amalek prevailed*" (Exodus 17:11 NASB). Moses eventually became weary and could no longer hold up his own arms. Aaron and Hur held his arms up for him until the Israelites defeated the Amalekites.

We must counter the lies of the enemy in godly communities, complimenting one another, not competing. Brave, but not prideful, transparent with dignity, kind and not judgmental. Second Corinthians 12:9 (NIV) says, *"But [Jesus] said to me, 'My grace is sufficient for you, for my power is made perfect in weakness.' Therefore I will boast all the more gladly about my weaknesses, so that Christ's power may rest on me."* When we show up in all seasons and all forms with women who love God and love us, they will hold up our arms, cover us in battle, and petition Heaven alongside us for victory and glory to God through our stories.

Lies Sound Like...

Lies will trap us, diminish us, and isolate us. Lies distance us from what God is doing and has done. **Every hurt or limitation in our lives is rooted in a lie from the enemy.** When we believe a lie, we allow it to distort behavior by distracting us, limiting us, and distancing us from who God is and what He is doing. Here's what they can sound like, but I encourage you to write out your own:

Lie 1: No one will ever understand_________, and no one else struggles with this.

Lie 2: If people knew the truth, they wouldn't like or accept me. They would think I was __________.

Lie 3: I will always be this way. My mom was like this, her mom was like this… it's just who I am.

Lie 4: I will never be free of __________. No matter how hard I try, I always come back to this. What does it matter?

Lie 5: I don't deserve anything more than what I have. Who would love me or want me?

Lie 6: God is good, but He isn't good to me.

Lie 7: Because of ___________, I am no longer worthy or qualified for my dream. This is my consequence.

Lie 8: Everyone else has it all together. I need to do it better- like __________.

Lie 9: I feel __________, so it must be true.

Lie 10: God can't or won't use me because ____________.

Often, it seems that Satan wants to distract us long enough to doubt the goodness, provision, and truth of God. Our enemy leads us to give into our selfish desires, fulfilling opposing values from what God has for us. In turn, we find ourselves on a path we never wanted to be on, in a story we never wanted to be in. There is a war against us. God created Eve from the very beginning as *ezer kenegdo* (helpmeet)—one who aids, who responds to cries for help. Before she ever said or did anything, her very namesake carried deep purpose.

The same is true for me, and for you. **We don't need anything more than what we have right now to be who God has called us to be.** God designed us with purpose, greatness, and precision. In His design, the Father gifted each one of us the very things we need to overcome the fight and rise victoriously with Him. **Victory will always depend on whether we fight with Him or without Him.** It's a choice to be obedient. It's a choice to trust His direction explicitly, and confidently proclaim that God has the final word. The battle has already been won and victory belongs to our God, but at times He calls us to fight.

The Fight Matters

There are going to be days and moments when you do not feel like prayerfully and intentionally engaging the unseen battle. It's easier to engage in the physical battle where symptoms are manifesting— battles with your parents, your husband, your children, coworkers, a friend, or anyone other than the real enemy. It's easier to respond to and engage the supposed problem. Why? They are right in front of us, clearly causing the issue, or so it seems. If you are like me, you hear and see the surface problem, and in about three seconds, you have a full response and solution built in your head. Before the issue is even finished, you have a solution formulated and a frustration backing it. It is only the first problem.

Our enemy wants us to feel like the victim, analyzing all the details of what we are seeing and experiencing, distracting, and exhausting us. The best thing we can do when days like this arise is to pause and to assess what fight we are engaging in. When we realize we are being played by the enemy, it's a choice to step into the unseen battle. We must pray for God's guidance, protection, and wisdom, and take up the right weapons that will change everything. When we fight the right fight, it impacts the root of a problem far more than if we had navigated it in our own strength and limitations.

The more we train and fight by encountering Him daily through His word and presence, the easier it becomes to detect the lies. The more we refine our skills and learn to see warning flags, the stronger we become as a spiritual daughter. Like any muscle exercised and strengthened over time, suiting up, submitting, and waiting on the Lord will become a natural posture for us. **If Eve can be led astray in a perfect world, we are at risk every day in an imperfect one.**

Called to Freedom

You, my brothers and sisters, were called to be free. But do not use your freedom to indulge the flesh; rather, serve one another humbly in love.
— Galatians 5:13 NIV

God calls us daughter (2 Corinthians 6:18). In the Greek text, the word "called" is *kaleo,* meaning "to invite, to receive as a name, to call loudly." Once we give our heart to the Lord, we receive a new identity and a new name: daughter. Our new name is superior to any other title we have ever had or will ever hold. In this definition, I see women as daughters of the King, who stand out in the crowd. We no longer look, sound, or respond like the world, but we are set apart. We are no longer trapped inside our lives, our emotions, and our circumstances. Freedom belongs to us because we are daughters of the King. What was once holding us back no longer holds a grip on us.

Regardless of where we are at in our lives, what we have done, and what we are walking through, know that God has called us to freedom. He has given us a new identity, not just for us to keep to ourselves, but to impact others for His glory. Freedom is the victory banner that He waves over us. Freedom is in His voice, the message He wants us to hear amongst the crowd. It is a new identity amidst our circumstance. Amid our season, He calls to us loudly that His yoke is easy (Matthew 11:30). He promises that He will never leave us (Deuteronomy 31:8). He promises that He has plans for our lives and that they are for good (Jeremiah 29:11). He calls us to freedom through a relationship with Him.

I am one person. If every woman is in a battle, we need other women to rise up. We need warriors who are going to battle for other women, introducing them to Jesus, helping them find freedom through relationship with Him.

We were created as warriors from the beginning. Remember, we stand in opposition when needed and we respond to cries for help. That is who we are, at our very core. We have been called to freedom, but never with the intent of freedom only for ourselves, but for everyone in our lives—freedom to impact, to love, to serve, and to lead others to Jesus.

Prayer

Thank You, Lord, that You are doing a new thing. Even from the beginning, You have had a special call on my life. Reflecting back, I can identify ways You have protected and covered me. Lord, I pray for false identities to be dropped, idols to be revealed, and the chains of bondage to culture, value, and striving to be broken in Jesus' name. Search my mind, God. Starve out anything in my mind that is not of you and allow a new mindset to rise as I begin to see myself as a kingdom warrior for You. I pray that no weapon formed against me prospers. In Jesus' name, I pray for wisdom to engage the right battles against the real enemy. Victory belongs to You. Purpose and worth are given to me because I have been created and called by You, and there is nothing I can do to earn that or lose that. Father, help me to walk confidently forward in this new identity! In Jesus' name, amen.

Discussion Questions

1. What are you carrying that God never intended for you to carry?

2. What lie(s) has the enemy targeted you with?

3. What examples can you think of where you have fought the wrong fight?

4. When reading Galatians 5:13, what does freedom mean and tangibly look like in your life? Who do you feel called to impact with your freedom?

3
The Armor of God

Be strong in the Lord and in his mighty power. Put on all of God's armor so that you will be able to stand firm against all strategies of the devil. For we are not fighting against flesh-and-blood enemies, but against evil rulers and authorities of the unseen world, against mighty powers in this dark world, and against evil spirits in the heavenly places.
— Ephesians 6:10-12 NLT

As a martial artist for over ten years, I have engaged in multiple sparring matches, physical contact fighting with pads and helmets, and I have realized that there is a strong parallel that we can make between a physical fight and the spiritual one. While we don't see or hear a war around us, we can begin to identify the characteristics of war as they manifest through thoughts and emotions to provoke action. In Ephesians, Paul writes a letter of encouragement and caution to the church in Ephesus to seek unity in the church, and that anyone who comes to Christ is accepted by God, endowed by the Holy Spirit. Chapter six is the foundation of Ephesians because it cautions, encourages, and equips believers far past what is seen. These attacks are conducted by Satan and his dark angels, seeking access into our minds to gain a foothold, a place of residence. Their attempts are pursued with the hope that over time we will perceive their lies as truth. **Ultimately, like Eve, if we can doubt God's instruction, then we create distance in our relationship with Him.** If we believe the Bible is the Word of God, that His Word stands the test of time, then we must respond to both the caution and the call to action of this unseen world's war.

But how? First, be strong in the Lord. This strength and courage do not come from us, how could it? We are humans, limited by our natural abilities, challenged by our reality daily. The Lord is where we draw strength and power from. Second, armor is essential. The phrase "put on" implies a level of intentionality and discipline that aligns us for success against the attacks. We are instructed to put on armor, which leads me to believe that

God has designed and positioned us with tools and resources to stand firm amidst whatever is targeting us. **A soldier would never enter battle without their protective gear, nor would a fighter enter a ring without the proper materials for success. Yet we go about our day, sometimes oblivious that we are fully exposed.** If it is crucial to our success to withstand, we need to know about this armor before we head out to our first battle.

With Paul's time in prison and his close contact with Roman soldiers, I tend to believe he correlated the attire of a Roman soldier, giving us a strong cultural visual and application.

The Armor of God

- The Belt of Truth
- The Breastplate of Righteousness
- The Shoes of Readiness from the Gospel of Peace
- The Shield of Faith
- The Helmet of Salvation
- The Sword of the Spirit

The Belt of Truth

Truth is an absolute stand by which reality is measured.
—Dr. Tony Evans, "A Spiritual Battle of Truth vs. Lies", *The Urban Alternative*

Truth—what is it these days? According to the Blue Letter Bible, the word "truth" in this passage is translated from the Hebrew word, *emeth* with the various meanings of stability, certainty, trust, assured, establishment, faithful, right, and sure. **Society will tell us that our truth is relative. Whatever we believe and whatever we feel, that should be right and true.** We have created our own truths, forsaking absolute truth, simply because it doesn't feel right, seem fair, or fit the narrative. If we believe the Bible to be true, Christ tells us in John 14:6 (NKJV) that *"I am* *the way, the truth, and the life."* Our truth lives, in the Word of God—for us, for our society, and for our world.

A Roman soldier suiting up would have started with the belt first. The belt was an essential core piece that attached and connected all of the other pieces of armor to move as intended. More importantly, the belt secured the sword. Roman soldiers were known to carry their swords in times of peace, but this belt could also sustain the momentum of a soldier running full speed ahead to engage his enemy. In some circumstances, the belt had leather strips that hung down that also offered protection to the lower part of the body. Whether a Roman soldier or a martial artist heading out to spar, every piece is applied with strategic placement and intention of protection in preparation for an oncoming attack.

> *Stand therefore, having girded your waist with truth.*
> — Ephesians 6:14 NKJV

In the same way, truth is our daily guiding force, our filter that everything else must attach to, the core piece. Without truth in our minds or our hearts, our thoughts, emotions, and actions are independent of one another. All aspects are left reactive to circumstances and relationships because they are disconnected to anything of stability or true security. When we are anchored to absolute truth, we can discern the slightest attacks of the enemy. Like a lie detector, God's truth is our filter to interpret and engage conversations, encounters, and scenarios with a heavenly response.

Money experts don't spend their time studying counterfeits. They study and interact with real money so much that when they touch a counterfeit, they know something is off. The feeling and look are different. The dollar responds differently. It's close, but it isn't the real thing. We need to be in the Word of God daily, knowing His Word, allowing it to penetrate deep within us. We need to know His heart and His characteristics so that when the lie comes, we pause because it is different from what we have known to be true. When the opportunity arises, when the temptation occurs, when the feelings are high and the season is tough, we pause. When the grief is unbearable, when the world tells us something that doesn't match Scripture, we pause. We compare it to the truth of God's Word and move forward from there. Not because the problem is resolved. Not because the healing has come, or the answer has arrived. We move forward because we trust a personal relationship with our heavenly Father. We rest in His truth and in all His ways.

We stand confident that we know who holds our every moment. We know and proclaim that God has a plan for our lives and His plan is for good. We know that He cares for us, that He designed us with a purpose from the beginning in our mothers' wombs. We stand fully aware of the battle waging around us. We can approach every season, circumstance, and random thing that arises with confidence that we wage war victoriously in Him.

Scriptures on Truth

> *Therefore each of you must put off falsehood and speak truthfully to your neighbor, for we are all members of one body. "In your anger do not sin": Do not let the sun go down while you are still angry, and do not give the devil a foothold.* — Ephesians 4:25-27 NIV
>
> *Make me know Your ways, O LORD; Teach me Your paths. Lead me in Your truth and teach me, For You are the God of my salvation; For You I wait all the day.* — Psalm 25:4-5 NASB
>
> *All the ways of the LORD are loving and faithful toward those who keep the demands of his covenant.* — Psalm 25:10 NIV
>
> *Sanctify them by Your truth. Your word is truth.* — John 17:17 NIV
>
> *All Scripture is God-breathed and is useful for teaching, rebuking, correcting and training in righteousness, so that the servant of God may be thoroughly equipped for every good work.*

—2 Timothy 3:16- 17 NIV

Do not let kindness and truth leave you;
Bind them around your neck,
Write them on the tablet of your heart.
So you will find favor and a good reputation
In the sight of God and man. — Proverbs 3:3-4 NASB

The Breastplate of Righteousness

The most basic element of any successful fighter is their stance. Before movement happens in a fight, two things need to happen:

1- Hands are brought up in a fist beside your cheekbones to guard and protect your face

2- Elbows are tucked in tight to protect your ribs and vital organs from injury

Similarly, no soldier would ever enter battle without a covering to protect their chest. Yet, day in and day out, we go into battle. We enter the fight in our own ways, our own strength, and our own good deeds with the hope of victory. It's hard enough to fight battles with our families and other real challenges, let alone withstand the attacks from a force we cannot see and barely understand. It simply isn't possible in the realm of our human limitations. We will fall short every time, because we have left our most vital area, our chest, exposed. As the Scriptures caution, "*Above all else, guard your heart, for everything you do flows from it*" (Proverbs 4:23 NIV).

In the simplest of terms, righteousness means right living in the laws of God's love and doing what is right in His eyes, not ours. Due to the fall, we are all born with sin. If you have spent any time with young children, you quickly see that sin is not something you have to teach, but something that naturally comes forth on its own, we are all born into it. When we go to fight spiritual, powerful forces that are both unseen and unknown to us without God's covering, any attack can knock us off balance and deeply wound us in ways that only His protection and barrier can heal us from.

It is not by accident that God gave the breastplate the attribute of righteousness, it covers and protects our most vital organ, physically and spiritually speaking—our heart. Everything we do flows from the heart. With His breastplate, sin and various attacks may scratch it, or even dent it, but they won't penetrate our heart. When we identify our lives and our allegiance in his army, we signal to the world which team we play for. Putting on the breastplate of righteousness identifies and unifies us with the laws and love of our Father. Without it, we are left unidentified as independent agents by the world, lost in the mix, separated from God.

By putting on His breastplate of righteousness, a right way of living, we can stand on any battlefield with confidence and hope. We can stand in seasons and circumstances that otherwise would have crushed us. We can stand with love and kindness. We can stand in joy. We can stand in peace with patience, gentleness, and self-control. Why? Because we have His armor. We are suited with the attributes of Christ that allow us to live and fight differently. And because He tells us that the battle has already been won. We are protected and guided through His laws in His Word.

Scriptures on Righteousness

In the way of righteousness is life, and in its pathway there is no death. — Proverbs 12:28 NASB

My tongue shall speak of Your word, for all Your commandments are righteousness. — Psalm 119:172 NKJV

Sober up morally and stop sinning, for some have no knowledge of God. I say this to your shame. — 1 Corinthians 15:34 NASB

Your righteousness is like the mountains of God; Your judgments are like a great deep. O LORD, You protect man and beasts.
— Psalm 36:6 NASB

My mouth will tell of your righteous acts, of your deeds of salvation all the day, for their number is past my knowledge. — Psalm 71:15 ESV

Your righteousness, O God, reaches the high heavens. You who have done great things, O God, who is like you? — Psalm 71:19 ESV

For all of us have become like one who is unclean, and all our righteous deeds are like a filthy garment; and all of us wither like a leaf, and our iniquities, like the wind, take us away.
— Isaiah 64:6 NASB

The Shoes of Readiness from the Gospel of Peace

In a karate sparring match, you are advised to imagine your opponent attacking someone you love. Every punch, kick, and counter combination matters. To fight, you assume a ready position. Left foot facing forward toward your opponent and right foot back in a semi-lunge, perpendicular to your left. Your hands are up, and elbows tucked in tight. Once the fight begins, stay on the balls of your feet allowing you to alternate sides and glide as needed. Successful mobility is crucial—light on your feet, swiftly moving as the fight changes.

The stance and all the details of it present us ready for the fight ahead. The same can be said about spiritual warfare. Paul talks about putting on shoes of preparation that come from the gospel of peace. The application of these shoes positions us as believers to be ready to respond to whatever the call, whatever the season and circumstances we face.

Consider it all joy, brethren, when you encounter various trials, knowing that the testing of your faith produces endurance. And let endurance have its perfect result, so that you may be perfect and complete, lacking in nothing.
—James 1:2-4 NASB

Dictionary.com defines being ready as:

1. completely prepared or in fit condition for immediate action or use
2. duly equipped, completed, adjusted, or arranged, as for an occasion or purpose
3. willing

Ephesians 6:15 (NIV) says "*...and with your feet fitted with the readiness that comes from the gospel of peace.*" Readiness propels action. Readiness signals a level of preparation to move forward, a stance of being equipped for purpose.

It's not if hard times come, it's when. We are on the balls of our feet, ready to move, poised to glide in any direction from a place of peace, trusting His perfect will to be done. We rise amidst the challenges surrounding us and embrace who He has called us to be—whole, complete, and lacking nothing for His glory. We don't anticipate and respond in fear. We don't cower under anxiety and the limiting concerns of what could be. We don't plant our feet heavy with weight during what the world sees. Instead, **we live fully present from a stance of peace. We have the gospel of Christ. His promises make us ready to stand, to move, and to glide in battle. We fight because we know the truth.** We know who holds our every moment; we know that His plans are for good in our lives. We press on with confidence, knowing that He loves us far more than we can ever understand. We move forward with peace, knowing that He promises to never leave us nor forsake us. This battle will not bury us, but God will use it for His glory, He has won the war.

Scriptures on Readiness

Peacemakers who sow in peace reap a harvest of righteousness.
— James 3:18 NIV

The LORD gives strength to his people; the LORD blesses his people with peace. — Psalm 29:11 NIV

You will keep in perfect peace those whose minds are steadfast, because they trust in you. — Isaiah 26:3 NIV

You will go out in joy and be led forth in peace; the mountains and hills will burst into song before you, and all the trees of the field will clap their hands. — Isaiah 55:12 NIV

I have told you these things, so that in me you may have peace. In this world you will have trouble. But take heart! I have overcome the world. — John 16:33 NIV

But the Advocate, the Holy Spirit, whom the Father will send in my name, will teach you all things and will remind you of everything I have said to you. Peace I leave with you; my peace I give you. I do not give to you as the world gives. Do not let your hearts be troubled and do not be afraid. — John 14:26-27 NIV

Do not be anxious about anything, but in every situation, by prayer and petition, with thanksgiving, present your requests to God. And the peace of God, which transcends all understanding, will guard your hearts and your minds in Christ Jesus. — Philippians 4:6-7 NIV

The Shield of Faith

Roman soldiers carried shields, called *scutum.* They were often crafted from wood and leather pieces, glued together, and covered in metal. Shields were often the most impressive pieces, formed in a rectangle as tall as the soldier. They could conceal and protect a soldier's entire body from arrows and other projectiles when he knelt down behind it. Moreover, when an attack was coming, soldiers could connect their shields together to form a barrier above and around, creating an impenetrable wall.

...above all, [take] the shield of faith with which you will be able to quench all the fiery darts of the wicked one — Ephesians 6:16 NKJV

What is faith? Why does Paul write the phrase "above all" when he refers to it? The word "faith" is derived from the Hebrew and Greek word, *feyth,* to bind or to unite. *Strong's Concordance* says faith is a moral conviction of religious truth, or the truthfulness of God, especially reliance upon Christ for salvation. Assurance, belief, and fidelity.

Faith is the fourth piece of armor, but the first piece that we are to "take up" when attacks come. We now can safely pause, kneel, and hold our position to remain firm for protection, and to not lose ground. The other side may seem intimidating and loud. It may even be tempting to let our shield down, but don't.

If the attacks are too great, this is where the community, our fellow warriors, come in. Remember, Satan does not want us in a community. Satan uses negative relational tactics best against women. Encounters filled with lies, competition, comparison, and loneliness. We need our sister warriors. When the attacks are too great to bear, call your sisters on the right and left to connect their shields with yours. Connected and reinforced, we are covered on all sides, impenetrable, no longer alone. Even from the inside of this dark force, we have sisters showing up proclaiming, I'm in this with you!

Now faith is the substance of things hoped for, the evidence of things not seen
— Hebrews 11:1 NKJV

Our shields are our defense, not our weapons. **We are not to use our faith as our weapon against others, but as our guard for refuge amid the battle.** If we begin fighting with our shields, hurling religion, judgement, and self-righteousness on others, we lose our coverage and protection. God extends grace to us and states clearly that judgement is His. The enemy is out to attack everyone, showing no favoritism to anyone. The enemy attacks us in countless ways. Division in our homes. Strife with our husbands and children, tension with coworkers, friends, and even fellow believers. **A divisive mindset is a win for the enemy.** We are not the law. We are not the judge. He is. Be tenacious with your faith, hold your position, and keep your shield in position to protect and defend when those arrows come.

Scriptures on Faith

So that your faith might not rest in the wisdom of men but in the power of God. — 1 Corinthians 2:5 ESV

For we walk by faith, not by sight. — 2 Corinthians 5:7 ESV

And without faith it is impossible to please God, because anyone who comes to him must believe that he exists and that he rewards those who earnestly seek him. — Hebrews 11:6 NIV

Because you know that the testing of your faith produces perseverance. — James 1:3 NIV

I have chosen the way of faithfulness; I have set my heart on your laws. — Psalm 119:30 NIV

For it is with your heart that you believe and are justified, and it is with your mouth that you profess your faith and are saved.
— Romans 10:10 NIV

The Helmet of Salvation

In martial arts, we spar with pads and a helmet, but I have taken some blows that knocked the wind out of me. One blow to the head (not allowed in karate), even with a padded helmet, could send one off balance or down, but with no helmet— I can't imagine the damage. I have engaged in many sparring matches with multiple attackers. Never once would I have stepped onto the mat to fight without a helmet.

The unseen battle that Paul refers to is raging around us daily. We can leave our helmet on the shelf while we fight with our own ability, our own strength forgetting our God-given freedom. I used to think salvation was a one-time thing. I viewed it like a formula: accept Christ, get baptized, then carry around your salvation card like a driver's license to share with people when they ask, “Yep, I’m saved. See my card?” Salvation is a daily gift. Salvation is an ongoing relational exchange with God, reminding us that we no longer live in our past actions or identities. We are no longer slaves to feelings, thoughts, and emotions. We no longer go out to battle unprotected and exposed in our own limiting beliefs and lies. No, we have a new identity in Christ. **Through salvation, we access freedom, new ways of thinking, hope, grace, and a deep purpose for our lives.**

By thinking salvation was a one-time thing versus a daily application, I was limiting myself and the very freedom Christ came to give. I received my helmet, but I wasn’t putting it on. Instead, I let it sit idle on a shelf. I should have put on my helmet when I responded poorly or allowed anger to get the best of me. My helmet should have been on when I extended judgement towards someone and chose not to forgive. I should have worn my helmet when I gave value and weight to my idols, things like success, money, and relationships. My past actions were justified with Christ. They were paid for, done, and no longer mine to carry. When Jesus died on that cross and I accepted Him as my Savior, I released those things and chose to let Him rule in my life so that I might be fully alive, and free. I was given a tool—a helmet.

If you declare with your mouth, "Jesus is Lord," and believe in your heart that God raised him from the dead, you will be saved. For it is with your heart that you believe and are justified, and it is with your mouth that you profess your faith and are saved. — Romans 10:9-10 NIV

Daily we need to put on and take with us our salvation because we are still sinners in need of a Savior.

Scriptures on Salvation

He put on righteousness as a breastplate, and a helmet of salvation on his head; he put on garments of vengeance for clothing, and wrapped himself in zeal as a cloak. — Isaiah 59:17 ESV

For by grace you have been saved through faith. And this is not your own doing; it is the gift of God, not a result of works, so that no one may boast. — Ephesians 2:8-9 ESV

Then he brought them out and said, "Sirs, what must I do to be saved?" And they said, "Believe in the Lord Jesus, and you will be saved, you and your household." — Acts 16:30-31 ESV

Because, if you confess with your mouth that Jesus is Lord and believe in your heart that God raised him from the dead, you will be saved. For with the heart one believes and is justified, and with the mouth one confesses and is saved. — Romans 10:9-10 NIV

Truly my soul finds rest in God; my salvation comes from him.
— Psalm 62:1 NIV

The Sword of the Spirit

Karate is a form of self-defense. The teaching is there to kill, if need be, but it is first and foremost a means of protection, not a weapon. The sword is the last piece of armor to "take up." In the Roman army, the sword, the *gladius*, was an incredible weapon, sharpened on both sides, designed to pierce even through metal. The sword is our first weapon. The other pieces are all for our defense and protection. The sword is what we fight with. "*Take the helmet of salvation, and the sword of the Spirit, which is the word of God"* (Ephesians 6:17 NIV).

Ephesians 6 tells us that the Spirit is the Word of God—the living Word, inspired by God. In spiritual warfare, nothing of our flesh or human creation will be of use to fight battles, only the living Word of God. A Roman soldier's sword was held and suspended by their belt. Don't miss this! Remember, truth is our belt. **If our belt of truth is off, flawed, or broken, I would challenge the capability of correctly carrying and supporting our sword as we run into battle.** Would you trust your weapon to be secure as the fiery arrows are flying by as you rush through busy days?

For the word of God is living and powerful, and sharper than any two-edged sword, piercing even to the division of soul and spirit, and of joints and marrow, and is a discerner of the thoughts and intents of the heart. And there is no creature hidden from His sight, but all things are naked and open to the eyes of Him to whom we must give account.
— Hebrews 4:12-13 NKJV

As I write this, the Lord has continued to bring me back to Luke 4 saying, "Read it again Danielle." Initially, I was studying verses 18-19, but after backing up a few verses, I noticed that the Spirit led Jesus into the wilderness. After forty days, Jesus became hungry. The devil tempted Jesus three different ways, all with things that in our flesh are desirable: food, dominion and authority, and power. In each temptation, Jesus only responded with Scripture. He didn't reason with the devil. He didn't clarify. He simply spoke the truth. Finally, Satan left, "*he left Him until an opportune time*" (Luke 4:13 NASB).

Jesus modeled the sword perfectly. Fighting attacks from the enemy with the Word of God, He triumphed. Satan had nothing else to give. If you notice in verse 13, Satan had to leave to build more strategies for a different time; his plans had failed. We are called to be warriors, so it is only fitting that God would give us the best weapon there is to fight. This is why it's crucial to truly know the Word of God and utilize it as our first attack when the battle arises inside us, with our spouse, our kids, our school, or at our work. Our sword, and the only weapon we are to use, is the Word of God.

Scriptures on the Word and Spirit

Be diligent to present yourself approved to God as a workman who does not need to be ashamed, accurately handling the word of truth.
— 2 Timothy 2:15 NASB

Let the word of Christ richly dwell within you, with all wisdom teaching and admonishing one another with psalms and hymns and spiritual songs, singing with thankfulness in your hearts to God.
— Colossians 3:16 NASB

So will My word be which goes forth from My mouth; it will not return to Me empty, without accomplishing what I desire, and without succeeding in the matter for which I sent it. — Isaiah 55:11 NASB

It is the Spirit who gives life; the flesh profits nothing; the words that I have spoken to you are spirit and are life. — John 6:63 NASB

All Scripture is inspired by God and profitable for teaching, for reproof, for correction, for training in righteousness; so that the man of God may be adequate, equipped for every good work.
— 2 Timothy 3:16 -17 NASB

Pray in the Spirit

When Jesus died on the cross a veil was torn in two from top to bottom, creating direct access to our Heavenly Father every single day (Matthew 27:51). After Jesus ascended to Heaven, we were given the gift of the Holy Spirit or "the Helper" to live and dwell within us. When we receive the Holy Spirit, and then begin to pray in the Spirit something special happens. The Spirit who is part of the Father and now with us prays on our behalf in a special way to the Father. This is a much bigger topic, but the important takeaway are these two points:

1- Praying in the Spirit is essential to victory in spiritual warfare

2- To grow in prayer, spend time with the Father daily asking Him speak to you and to give you your prayer language

Praying in the Spirit is a supernatural exchange. A relational encounter beyond our ability to understand or control, a personal language available to everyone!

Taking up God's armor sets you apart in a world that is dark and confusing. Putting on His armor models hope and steadfast guidance to a culture that is lost in the shuffle of relative truth, a truth reactive to feelings and circumstances. You are no longer that person. No longer do you walk that path, think that way, or respond as the world might. You belong to His light, and as such, are called to be the light. Look at these two verses:

> *Besides this you know the time, that the hour has come for you to wake from sleep. For salvation is nearer to us now than when we first believed. The night is far gone; the day is at hand. So then let us cast off the works of darkness and put on the armor of light.... But put on the Lord Jesus Christ, and make no provision for the flesh, to gratify its desires.* — Romans 13:11-12, 14 ESV

> *But you are not in darkness, brothers, for that day to surprise you like a thief. For you are all children of light, children of the day. We are not of the night or of the darkness. So then let us not sleep, as others do, but let us keep awake and be sober. But since we belong to the day, let us be sober, having put on the breastplate of faith and love, and for a helmet the hope of salvation.*
> — 1 Thessalonians 5:4-6, 8 ESV

Prayer:

Thank you, Lord, for this armor. Out of your deep love for me, you are not only guiding me, but equipping me along the way for a victory that brings You glory. You have entrusted me, Your daughter with the most powerful resources and weapons of warfare. Guide my mind, guide my heart, continue to train my hands. Forgive me when I have forgotten to surrender my battles to You or forgotten to put on Your armor. Your mercies are new each day, so every day, every moment, I thank you that I can suit up anytime. In Jesus' name I rebuke a spirit of shame that works against my efforts and thoughts to pursue the right fight in alignment with Your heart. Guard me, Father. Help me to remember that the best thing I can do is rest in You, Your Word, and Your truths! I love you, Lord. Amen.

Discussion Questions:

1. When you read Ephesians 6:10-12, what comes to mind for you?
2. What does truth mean to you?
3. What stuck out most to you about the application of armor?
4. If someone were to assess your armor for battle, what would they say?
5. What is one thing you can begin doing differently with your armor?

4
The Battle Against Our Heart

Above all else, guard your heart, for everything you do flows from it.
— Proverbs 4:23 NIV

Our Hearts

The heart is the epicenter of all that we do. Every day our hearts pump two thousand gallons of blood to our five vital organs. Our hearts affect everything in our bodies, and the opposite is also true—everything impacts our hearts from what we eat to the emotions we have. Symbolically, our hearts possess our greatest desires, fears, pains, regrets, hopes, and dreams. Maybe that's why this organ has been assigned with emotion due to the electrical response, or maybe it's because it's the lifeline to everything else.

To build anything, we must have a strong foundation or all else is subject to fail. You see, when God created us, He made each of us in His image. God only operates in perfection. Our hearts are also created after His, for worship, community, and love. Remember those best friend necklaces? When we grow in relationship with the Father and align our hearts to what His heart wants and commands, our hearts find their other half. We experience wholeness.

If you have ever tried to run a marathon, or even half a mile and any part of your body is injured, you will be hindered until it is resolved or healed. In the same way, we will struggle greatly to build strength, increase capacity, gain efficiency, or endure impact if our hearts are weak or broken.

Throughout my life, I have made many decisions led by strong emotional responses rooted in my heart's deepest desires. A desire to be seen, truly loved, and fully known. Truth be told, I have hopped aboard way too many emotional roller coasters and taken along more passengers than I care to admit in my pursuit for my hearts desires—family, friends, boyfriends, etc. A crazy rush of emotions would come over me, prompting me to respond. Within moments, I would formulate a solution and act impulsively, almost as if operating unconsciously. At times, I would catch myself going through the motions, sometimes very irrational ones. It never occurred to me to wait or pray through any of it. I pressed on, most of the time to the detriment of myself and any relationship I was involved in. **God places those desires in our hearts, but when we place those God-given desires in the wrong hands, anything of great value or importance can become a weapon against us.**

Looking back my heart was wounded. Instead of taking my wounded heart to the Healer, I applied bandages after family hurts, and more bandages after break ups. I quickly put band aids on hurtful friendships and events that I had placed great expectations upon. Here I was showing up to new seasons of my life, taking on new "good things" with the intent of a marathon distance, but the heart capacity of a 5K at best. My heart's deepest desires were blocked by hurt and bitterness. I continued to place expectations for healing from people, and not from the Father. Externally portraying confidence and happiness, most of the time I felt I was crumbling internally, exhausted, and losing hope. After years of band aids and masks to cover up the hurt, and failed attempts for healing, I realized something profound after reading this quote from Brené Brown:

I performed until there was no energy left to feel. I made what was uncertain certain, no matter what the cost. I stayed so busy that the truth of my hurting and my fear could never catch up. I looked brave on the outside and felt scared on the inside.

— Brené Brown, *Daring Greatly*

After reading Brown's words, I saw myself for the first time with complete clarity. I needed healing that neither I, nor someone else could give. I had allowed hurt things to become broken things and broken things to become identity. The broken lens became my value lens; I saw myself as broken. In the attempt to cover and heal, I never addressed the roots of the hurt. My deepest desires became my deepest wounds.

The Battle against Our Hearts

Many forms of martial arts advance in ranks through the earning of belts (colored fabric) worn around the waist of the student. The day had arrived for my advanced purple belt test. Sparring, or fighting full contact with pads on, was the last event of the day, and I was not looking forward to it.

"BEGIN!" The instructor called out, and two opponents got up to fight. I maneuvered quickly around the mat, throwing counter attacks as I could. Minutes in, another joined. Then another, and another. Five suited and advancing attackers worked me around the mat, attempting to corner me and make contact in the fight, pushing me to every limit. Exhausted and weak, I desperately would have given anything for fellow students to come to my aid. Glancing over, I desired for spectators to join in and help fight the attackers for a triumphant victory, or at least relief. Instead, with tears streaming down my face and a bloody nose, I struggled to move around the mat alone. Low on energy and strength, I sloppily threw punches and kicks, anything to keep my opponents back. As soon as the bell rang, I knew it would all be over. *Just hang in there, Danielle, it's almost over.*

This external experience became a concept I would revisit often. This idea of transparency, relief, authentic relationships, and breakthrough. Maybe you can relate, going around the mat while the blows are coming, desperately looking on for a fellow friend to step in and offer help. I wanted to become a black belt, but I had to go through the various belts and tests to receive it.

If everything flows from our hearts, then every battle originates in our hearts. Every dream, fear, desire, failure—we feel them. They impact us because they flow from our hearts. Satan took God's words in the garden of Eden, tempted Eve with fruit, and proposed something that spoke to her heart. More. The ability to be like God, to have knowledge, to know good and evil. Remember, the tactics haven't changed.

My heart's greatest desires through ten years of failed relationships, empty pursuits, and value-filled earthly chases were a pursuit for affirmation. For a long time I placed blame on people and experiences for what happened, but that didn't help, nor did the blame ever bring healing to unlock those deepest desires.

Maybe you were raised in an environment that didn't give you what you needed. Maybe those closest to you were never given the tools and truth they needed to fight their own fights to get past lies and hurts. All this can change with me, and with you, today. Right here. Right now. We may not be able to change what happened previously, but we can change the course ahead. Change begins with our hearts.

We've Been Played

God has seen and walked alongside each of us our entire story. Every season of abundance and drought, God was there. Every scar and every victory, God has been there.

Satan has also been observing. Looking back, I realize now that I was being played, and unknowingly, I played right into it. The enemy was setting bait for me in seasons and places, and I fell for it, almost every time. When I allowed hurt and brokenness to reside, I allowed a foothold for the enemy. It's only a matter of time until he wrecks complete havoc. My heart's desire for an authentic relationship was the very thing the enemy twisted and tempted me with as a distraction from the right thing. The relationship in front of me looked good, sounded good, and felt right, so I gave in. Relationships became my idol. I chose to pursue immediate gratification, instead of God's promises, resting in His process, waiting for His best.

When the hurt or heartbreak happened, I quickly pursued the next high, hoping that it would fix and heal enough of whatever was wrong to get me through to happier times. Satan must have loved watching me spiral. While I felt stuck, broken, confused, and lonely, I never once paused to look at it differently. Now I can see God was at work. Through my pain, He was persistently inviting me into a true relationship with Him. When God does something, He doesn't simply check the box and move on. He calls us His masterpiece, so there is nothing short of excellence, majesty, and expertise that He pours out over us when we surrender to Him.

I wanted to be truly happy; God wanted me to be truly healed. Always a learner of things the hard way, I wish I could tell you I realized the enemy's tactic after a year or two of toxic life cycles, but I didn't. Instead, I tried to outwork and outperform everything and everyone, determined to fix it, alone.

As in water face reflects face, so the heart of man reflects the man.

— Proverbs 27:19 ESV

Remember, everything flows from the heart. If our hearts are weak or broken, then our ability to see, assess, and accurately fight is compromised. If we have given access unknowingly to the enemy, then we must evict him immediately for healing to take place. Period. No questions. No exceptions.

God-given Desires Rest in God-given Promises

Each dream and desire, at its root, is from the Lord—the desire to have a greater relationship with our spouse; the desire to be seen and accepted by others; the desire to protect and provide for those we love; the desire to have purpose, and worth, and to be validated. **We can't obtain full satisfaction in what we deeply desire without first having a relationship with our Creator, then working towards healing and health in our lives.**

I truly believed my challenges would be resolved if I figured out the right formula or worked harder towards whatever I desired. I often thought that when I found the right person, then it would all be fixed. If you aren't married, spoiler alert—marriage doesn't fix anything. Marriage is a partnership that provides a raw transparent lens to magnify everything each of you have carried and are walking through now. What's inside comes out. Unhealed hurts get exposed. Good things get better, and hard things become harder.

One night, I surrendered. I had just broken up with a boyfriend, and I was tired on all levels. Priscilla Shirer delivered a message, and I realized I needed to own my healing and change if I wanted my future to look differently. With tears streaming down my face, I silently prayed, "I am so tired of this pattern and this place. How is it that ten years later, I am still here— single, broken, tired, and feeling lost?! I don't want to come back to this 'place' ever again God! If that means doing it Your way now and letting go of what I want most, take it. I will give it to You completely." That night, I set out on a new path for my life. I made new commitments to myself and to Jesus and established personal boundaries to help me begin to live differently.

It didn't make sense. I stopped pursuing what my heart desired most in my own ways, gave God my heart, my desires, my fears, and all my hurts and trusted Him to begin the healing process. In all honesty, I expected to feel lonely, and sad that what I desired most, I just gave up. The opposite happened. That very week with my heart surrendered to the Father, and my eyes focused on His healing and work in my life, I began to experience more joy, fulfillment, and wholeness than I ever had before. Here's what changed, my deepest desires, the ones He gave me had finally been placed back in the hands of my loving Creator and were no longer a weapon that could be used against me. God was able to provide the truth, healing, and growth to which I deeply needed to anchor... The only One who could speak to my heart, to my greatest desires because He created and designed me. The only One who was able to help me find perspective, wholeness, and true joy, even when the circumstances and seasons still looked bleak. Trusting Him and pursuing a relationship with Him gave me a peace that didn't make sense to the outside world amidst circumstances that hadn't changed. But my heart had been awakened to more with Christ. **There is never a better solution for a broken, lost, or hurt heart than being in the loving hands of our Creator.**

Satan, 100 percent, does not want us to know this wholeness and healing for our hearts. Why? Because dropping the heavy, suffocating, and limiting chains of identity and baggage of the world in exchange for God's promises of true love, peace, rest, protection, provision, and freedom is life changing. We won't ever want to go back. Try as the enemy or his demons might, as free women we become exponentially harder to recapture.

The more our hearts align with Christ, the more easily we move through battle while under His covering. We gain a new, heavenly perspective in every battle, giving us the ability to remain grounded in strength and peace while engaging onward. I said easily move… not to be confused with an easy life. Following Jesus and walking daily with Him doesn't mean we are trial free. In contrast, James 1:2-4 (NASB) says, "*Consider it all joy, my brethren, when you encounter various trials, knowing that the testing of your faith produces endurance. And let endurance have its perfect result, so that you may be perfect and complete, lacking in nothing.*" So be expectant. Be on alert. Things will happen. But stand confident that God has not left you, nor forsaken you. He is at work, and He has a purpose for your life as you weather storms. He wastes nothing—no person, no scar, no story, no experience. Trust your heart to Him. Ask Him to seek it, to test it, and to reveal to you what He has for you.

Victory rests with the Lord. — Proverbs 21:31 NIV

Healing

If you are in that place of needing some healing, I'm crazy proud of you for admitting that. It's hard and it's not a fun place to be. But you know what, you are already better for it, and that stance alone shines great courage in who you are becoming. Small steps forward can look like: praying, daily being in God's Word, going to counseling, reading helpful resources, or plugging into a small group at church. Begin to surround yourself with health, light, and His truth. **Don't give up on fighting for freedom. Remaining idle, doing nothing is the worst thing you can do in a fight.**

You will never regret investing in and fighting for who God has designed and called you to be.

Maybe your heart is in a healthy place, but you are looking for tools to fight the right fight. Regardless of where you are in your season or journey, there is a great next step here for you. I have listed Scriptures in *appendix 2* for you to keep close as His promises. Below is a four-step tool that I use as my battle strategy when I feel I am under attack.

Stand firm then, with the belt of truth buckled around your waist, with the breastplate of righteousness in place, and with your feet fitted with the readiness that comes from the gospel of peace. In addition to all this, take up the shield of faith, with which you can extinguish all the flaming arrows of the evil one. Take the helmet of salvation and the sword of the Spirit, which is the word of God. And pray in the Spirit on all occasions with all kinds of prayers and requests. With this in mind, be alert and always keep on praying for all the Lord's people.

— Ephesians. 6:14-18 NIV

Four Steps to Breaking the Lie

1. **Expose the lie.**
2. **Find God's truth.**
3. **Replace and rewrite the lie with truth.**
4. **Declare the new truth over your life.**

Expose the lie. Say it out loud or write it out but get it out so that it's in front of you and no longer in you.

Find God's truth to combat it. If no Scripture comes to mind, Google it: Scriptures on hope. Scriptures on healing. Promises of God.

Replace the lie with Scripture-based truth. The lie isn't dead. You have just stopped it momentarily. Here we create a new pathway in our mind. This can look like memorizing a verse, or creating a new statement, rooted in Scripture that we repeat over and over when the lie rears its head.

Declare the new truth. Proclaim it! Take your authority back. Thank God that the lie has been exposed and is breaking. With confidence, declare that breakthrough is coming, and victory belongs to the Lord! Worship, and believe that His promises are for you.

The following are examples of what the four-step battle strategy could look like:

1. **The Lie**—No one will ever love me and fully accept me if they know the real me.
2. **The Truth**—Even in the midst, God sees me and walks with me through every part of what hurts, and He still chose to give His Son so I can spend eternity with Him (Romans 5:8).
3. **The Replacement**—Love comes from You, God. I am seen, loved, and pursued by You. I replace the lie with the truth that I am Your daughter and in Your timing, You are making all things new, including me!
4. **The Declaration**—Today I declare that I am loved and seen by God. I break ties with these lies and the enemy's authority to disqualify me from the truth that God has promised. Your Word never returns void, God, so I declare that I am loved, that I am valued, and that the thing I want to hide most is the very thing You want to use most to bring you glory! I give it to You and remove all power and titles from it that are not from you.

1. **The Lie**—I am not worthy of what I desire… this is what I deserve.
2. **The Truth**—God only gives good gifts, and He is always faithful. If something hasn't happened, it is because in His mercy and grace He has more in store. He will bring it forth in His timing. *"For I know the plans I have for you," declares the Lord, "plans to prosper you*

and not to harm you, plans to give you hope and a future" (Jeremiah 29:11 NIV).

3. **The Replacement**—I am worthy and wanted by my heavenly Father. He desires a relationship with me, first and foremost. He is a good, faithful Father and knows the desires of my heart, so I will rest and seek Him in the waiting.
4. **The Declaration**—I break ties with shame and the lie of being unworthy of what I desire most. God, help me to desire You more than I desire anything else. In my waiting, help me to trust Your plan. You are my rest, You are my hope, and You are my joy. Satan, you have no authority here. In Jesus' name, you must leave; you have no place here and I no longer will accept your lies. God, I declare that You are working all things together for my good!

Practical Fighting Tip: Awareness

One of the most basic yet profound lessons found across all styles is awareness. When we pay attention to what and who is around us, we quickly begin to familiarize ourselves with what is happening and formulate a strategy for help, defense, or escape. This involves looking around as you walk, making eye contact with people as you see them, paying attention to surrounding details so you can easily detect when something seems odd or suspicious. To avoid being reactive to an attack, take in as many details as you can about your environment.

Awareness applies to our hearts, what is weighing on us, and what we are feeling. Be aware of all of it, take inventory of all things that are happening or things you are consuming, and present it all to the Lord. Darkness and heaviness cannot remain once exposed to the light.

Prayer

Thank You, Lord, that You created my innermost being. Before anything else, You designed my heart. You know the things deep inside my heart. Lord, search me today. Test me to expose anything not of You, so that You may uproot and refine anything in my heart. Anything that has taken or is trying to take root to rob me from Your best—bitterness, shame, guilt, anger, loss—I break ties with those today. As I surrender my heart to You, I ask that You bring healing to the hurt parts, areas where I have misplaced my deepest desires and I give them back to You. Thank You for Your word and Your promises. You are victorious. You have won this battle, and I declare freedom in You today. Give me a new heart and help me to love others as You would.

Discussion Questions

1. What is a dream or desire of your heart?
2. Where have you seen the enemy work to attack that dream or desire?
3. Pray and ask the Lord what He is asking you to do with that desire.
4. What lie, if any, needs to be replaced in your life?
5. Where do you need healing to take place in your heart to experience true freedom?

5
The Battle Against Our Mind

We are destroying speculations and every lofty thing raised up against the knowledge of God, and we are taking every thought captive to the obedience of Christ. — 2 Corinthians 10:5 NASB

Through my late twenties, I struggled with a stronghold of rejection. Almost instantly, my mind could recall events where feelings of rejection were triggered. Remember, Satan's strongest tactic is deception. When I wasn't paying attention to what was really happening, I unknowingly permitted past events and emotions to send me down a mental spiral. While feelings are valid, it's important to notice something I missed, authority and responsibility. Amid the thoughts and feelings, there is a responsibility and authority that 2 Corinthians 10:5 commands action. It's a choice, a choice I didn't know to make. **Left unaware of the strategy at play, I permitted thoughts to establish neural pathways and habits, which eventually led into new beliefs. Lies set in, and I began to believe them as my truths.**

Truth and Lies Blur Together

In my experience, a new action or belief in myself hasn't happened overnight, rather in the hundreds of small encounters and moments. When I permitted a lie to remain in my mind, I permitted an intruder. When we have an enemy in our midst, there are no boundaries. Working in deception, the enemy entangled fragments of lies to form a whole picture of "truth," making it seem right, as if all the supporting evidence was clear in my mind. Simultaneously at times, I would feel crazy as my thoughts and emotions could range so widely, often leaving me wondering how I could think or feel one way so strongly and just as quickly in the next feel as though I was falling apart. So often I felt like a mess, therefore I believed I was a mess.

The Battle Against Our Mind

For God has not given us a spirit of fear, but of power and of love and of a sound mind. — 2 Timothy 1:7 NKJV

If you love a good checklist like I do, here are three things that we must do when we sense a lie working to attack our minds:

1- Take Responsibility
2- Declare Truth
3- Step into Authority

We have a responsibility as believers to take inventory of everything working in our minds and compare it to God's Word. Second, as we compare it to His word, we must cling to that truth, not what we feel, not what our circumstances are telling us, or even what our minds are pushing, His truth. Lastly, we have authority and power as daughters of the King to take those thoughts captive and make them submit to His Word.

This battle has kicked my tail more often than I can count, and this whole submission to the Lord is something I must work at regularly... okay, like hourly. It is hard to take something that seems and feels both clear and straightforward, and still submit or lay it down for the Lord and wait for confirmation. If you struggle with that, like I do, that's ok. It means we are showing up to the fight, leaning in to learn so we can grow, exercising our spiritual muscles and minds for discipline. It's not OK to give up on the fight, to hear the narrative in our heads and simply receive that as truth. God has the final word. Before we are anything else, we are daughters of the one true God. Followers and disciples. That truth and identity is exalted above all else. The war for our minds, our identities and beliefs has been won. Navigating this battle begins with prayer, listening, intentionality, massive endurance, and relentless hope in the victory, knowing that His Word never fails!

Trapped in a Web

When I first wrote this section, my husband was traveling and unavailable to talk one evening, everyone seemed so busy. As feelings of loneliness moved in, lies like, "you don't matter to anyone" began to spring forth. Quickly realizing I wasn't processing this clearly and was entertaining an old stronghold of rejection; I took a stance to rebuke it and overcame it through prayer and worship. The heaviness broke, and I made the best of my evening. I wish all battles were that easy.

I am going to try and articulate the amount of spiritual warfare that has waged against me the whole week leading up to editing and revising this chapter. This battle went to a new level!

While Chris was deployed, communication was limited, more so than ever before. A situation occurred that we needed to talk through but had very little time and energy for. I presented the problem a few times to engage it, he thought things had been resolved and wanted to move on. Knowing I needed his attention in a way he couldn't give in that season, I put the issue on the shelf to talk about later. I'm sure you can guess how all this went down when he returned from the tour.

One evening after his return, I engaged the topic. Surprised, he thought things had been resolved, that I was past it, and it seemed unnecessary to bring up a situation for discussion. I was shocked. *How could he possibly think that?* Deployment reintegration has enough challenges of its own, but with this one there were minor things that transpired, continuing to drive us further apart. That evening a very real and low feeling of loneliness and concern set in. I needed my husband. We needed each other. Here we were at odds when we should have been "covering" the other in prayer and support, yet neither of us could get past our thoughts and frustration to show up for the other.

Day after day, I cried when circumstances stayed the same. For the first time in a long time, I felt trapped inside a web—able to see the outside, able to articulate what life outside of the web felt like, but unable to find my way out. There is always room for improvement in marriage, but we work hard at communication both efficiently and intentionally. Miscommunication and misunderstandings for seven long days simply isn't how we fight in our marriage.

Thoughts of past failed relationships surfaced in my mind. Lies flashed, prompting me to apply past formulas of failed relationships to my marriage. Fear spiraled. Logically, my husband and I were not just going to walk away and find what appeared to be "greener grass," but the enemy continued to yell differently in my mind. I struggled to quiet the lies. What if the deployment had changed him? What if this was our "new normal"? What if this pregnancy was too much for us emotionally? I hit my knees in prayer. I played worship music continuously. I prayed for breakthrough, for a light of hope. I prayed for relief from the warfare that felt like it was waging all around me. I couldn't pinpoint the direction of the fire. I couldn't see clearly; exhaustion was setting in—mentally and emotionally. Loneliness and vulnerability were the resounding feelings.

In need of breakthrough, I engaged a few of my "battle-buddies." These women came spiritually suited for battle! Each responded with texts or calls in total authority, fierce tenacity, and a fresh energy for the fight… things I no longer had, everything I desperately needed.

Remember, I was supposed to be working on this chapter. Every time I opened my computer to dive in, I closed it only to cry out to the Lord, "What is happening?! Where are You? Why are You not intervening?"

That night, Chris and I talked and went through it all. After I shared what I was carrying and what I felt like I was fighting against, he leaned in and said, "Let's pray together." As he prayed, Chris spoke against a spirit of rejection—rebuking it and demanding it to leave. He prayed with authority over our marriage, over our home, and over my mind. I felt something in my spirit shift. Something was breaking, the web was clearing.

Afterwards I sat quietly in bed thinking, *that's exactly what I have been fighting all week—a spirit of rejection! How did I miss this?!* Here's how—deception. The enemy was deceiving me to keep me focused on the wrong things at the wrong time with the wrong person through misunderstood encounters. Satan successfully had me running all week mentally and emotionally. My truth was so blurred with the lies that I couldn't find my way out. Even if I had seen the "right way out," I was tired.

The following day, a girlfriend encouraged me, "Danielle, I feel like the enemy wants to cripple you and for you to fail at this. If you fail, then you won't write a book to empower and encourage other women that they can rise victoriously too. I heard the Lord say, 'Don't give up, breakthrough is coming, press on.'" She was right and it lit a fire inside of me.

Here I was supposed to be working on this chapter that entire week. Yet, this was the very thing I felt like I was struggling with most. I was supposed to be sharing how to overcome it, but I couldn't even find my way out of it. Do I wish that week had gone differently? Yes. Did I learn a lot? Absolutely. Did I fail? No. I kept showing up, fighting in the best way I knew how. When the fight felt too much, I invited other female warriors in.

Make No Mistake

The battles against our minds may be different; but make no mistake, attacks will come. **God has given each of us a story, a voice, and a group of people who desperately need to hear about what Jesus has done and is doing through us.** Satan wants to silence us, disqualify us, and replace God's truth with lies. His tactics and strategies for deception and entry are always at work. Every season of our stories, every encounter or opportunity, we have a choice of whose truth we trust, whose promises we rest in, and how to engage forward.

Training and strategizing never stop in military life. Every week there are meetings. Monthly there are reports due, and regularly there are training events to keep soldiers trained, conditioned, and focused on the mission ahead. The mission may be one month or one year away, but there is no lack of clarity from the soldier who the enemy is and what mission success looks like.

God allowed me to walk this out in this way so I could tell you honestly that it isn't pretty. **Breakthrough and victory don't always come quickly and easily, rather through prayerful persistence to keep fighting.** Even the best, most trained fighters still struggle and work for every victory. It's imperative that we continue to show up and lean into the Father. We must continue engaging our various methods of defense, protection, and weapons in battle, rallying fellow warrior-sisters as new things try to rise up against us. Our minds are powerful places, and whatever we think is true, we are probably right. What we do with it and the outcome of it is up to us.

The more we spend time in His presence, the more familiar we are with truth to navigate the attack we are under. In each battle, we grow stronger when we listen to His call for us. Through testing, we become better equipped to avoid those old pitfalls and see with divine clarity what is happening in the background, past our emotions, and past what our minds are portraying as "truth."

Be alert and of sober mind. Your enemy the devil prowls around like a roaring lion looking for someone to devour. — 1 Peter 5:8 NIV

Be on guard. Stand firm in the faith. Be courageous. Be strong.
— 1 Corinthians 16:13 NLT

Overcomer

Sisters, we have spiritual and supernatural power to tear down strongholds in our lives. Anything previously built that we have grown to believe and rely upon, we have authority in Jesus to take it captive and make it submit to the truth of Christ.

After my first daughter was born, postpartum depression set in. Second Corinthians 10:3-5 became an anthem, a declaration of being an overcomer. While I felt paralyzed by fear, exhaustion, and loneliness, I walked. Twice a day, I pushed Emmaus in a stroller with tears streaming down my face, repeating over and over and over, "I am destroying everything that is raised up and setting itself up against the knowledge of Christ. I take every thought captive; you are under the obedience of Jesus Christ!" Something would break off a little, and I felt like I was coming up for a moment of air. "Ok, Danielle, you can do this. Go back inside and do the next thing. The day will be over soon. Thank You, Lord; another day done."

Life as a new mom was challenging; with a husband deployed, my circumstances seemed even more so. I was angry and was struggling against harboring bitterness. My emotions were real and valid, the world reminded me of that often. With no family nearby, my church family carried me during that season in countless ways. Satan would have loved nothing more than to have me seep further and further into a black hole, isolating myself from the world and disengaging from my husband.

I questioned everything. Things I thought were going to happen didn't, things I never thought would happen did. The lens through which I looked at my circumstances didn't add up much to the picture that continued to replay in my head. Right or wrong, it wasn't supposed to happen *this* way. For four months I struggled with depression and confusion about who I was, what I was doing, and how to find joy again. Things needed to change, but I wasn't sure how to do that.

Here's the thing, **we can either let life build us or bury us.** "*God has not given us a spirit of fear; but of power and of love and of a sound mind*" (2 Timothy 1:7 NKJV). We have spiritual warfare tools that we need to engage regularly, to tear this down. We have this power, the ability to have supernatural rest, peace, and strength as we trust in His victory. We must choose every day—does the world define my truth? Does the world define my circumstances? What about my limitations? Will I receive and proclaim my truth from God?

We align for victory when we focus our sight supernaturally, intentionally, and strategically on our Father, who knows us and designed us for purpose. My own parents didn't understand my battle and the specific ways the enemy was targeting me against what God had planted within me. Because of their natural, human love for me, they often empathized and grieved with me, "You have so much on your plate, you are in survival mode. This is an impossible season. I don't know how you are doing it." They love me and would do anything for me, but this wasn't their walk or their calling. It was mine. I had to own it, and you must own yours. Through prayer, worship, and continual declaration of God's truth over my mind, my feelings followed. One day the fog lifted. One day I was able to see with clarity and process that the season of heaviness was over and that I had overcome it.

There is more for you, friend. There is breakthrough and freedom. That is a promise from the Lord. We need to lead our minds in His truth until our feelings and circumstances follow.

People will probably never understand your walk, your battle, and your choices as you lay strongholds, toxic thoughts, lies, and lots of other junk at the foot of the cross. **Freedom doesn't make much sense to people that are still bound by chains, restricted by their own bars. They aren't the ones fighting for our best lives or our freedom; we are.** When we pursue freedom and the path God has for us, then we aren't in pursuit of worldly approval or answers. God designed each of us differently. He has called each of us differently. He has planted certain and specific things deep down inside of us that aren't in others, and that is ok. Overcoming any battle begins with the decision in our minds to fight and rise above both circumstances and environments to access a spiritual outpouring of an exchange with the ONE who made us.

The Power of Your Mind

Dr. Caroline Leaf, a communication pathologist and cognitive neuroscientist, is a brilliant Christian author and speaker on the power of renewing your mind in Romans 12:2. "*Do not conform to the pattern of this world, but be transformed by the renewing of your mind. Then you will be able to test and approve what God's will is—his good, pleasing and perfect will.*"

Thirty years ago, [Dr. Leaf] asked a ridiculous question... "*Can the mind change the brain?*" She embarked on a journey to study and apply it in her practice. In her talk, "Science of a Thought", she describes the formation of a thought:

> *If you study the brain, you can actually see...that as your thoughts are forming in the brain, they form on your neurons, and they look like trees. So, I really believe at that stage as you're using your mind, you can change your brain....Neuroplasticity means your brain can change,...but it has to be stimulated to change....We have a malleable brain...the more you actually direct your mind, the more your brain's going to grow. So, the harder you think; the deeper you think; the more you ask, answer, and discuss your information; the more you grow your brain; the more intelligent you become....No matter what kind of neurological, psychological impairment you have in your brain...by deep intellectual thinking, you can change your brain with your mind.*

Where people in the faith have sought to separate science, Dr. Leaf has made it her mission to prove the science through Scripture. Look at some of these facts below:

The *New Yorker* reported that "*our Memory is prioritized by emotion.*" If that's the case, when we recall a memory, the mind composes a story usually correlated to the highlights of an encounter or event that triggered the greatest rise of emotion. Our emotions are real, they matter. But what if I the things our minds may be relaying are only fragments of the truth?

87 to 95 percent of the illnesses that plague us today are a direct result of our thought life. What we think about affects us physically and emotionally. It's an epidemic of toxic emotions. —Dr. Caroline Leaf

If our mind is not right, the passions and excitement that God has laid inside of us will not come out and you will always be dissatisfied and walk around whiny and moany, complaining about all the things that have happened to us, turning around, wanting what everyone else has got, and you make a lousy them and an amazing you. If you keep whining and moaning about what everyone else has got, your brain is busy dying, it isn't designed for that. And since your brain controls your body, so your body is affected by what you are saying, thinking and doing

.—Dr. Caroline Leaf, "Detoxing Your Mind: An Interview With Dr. Caroline Leaf"

We must remain aware at all times of the thoughts we are thinking and make them submit to the truth of God's Word. Assess the root of what is happening and pray to see it with spiritual eyes so that you may know His truth. Second Corinthians 10:3-5 (NASB) lays it out clearly, "*For though we walk in the flesh, we do not war according to the flesh, for the weapons of our warfare are not of the flesh, but divinely powerful for the destruction of fortresses. We are destroying speculations and every lofty thing raised up against the knowledge of God, and we are taking every thought captive to the obedience of Christ.*"

After ten years of toxic thoughts and mindsets, I can't encourage you enough to pause and lean into the Father's heart on who He created you to be. Pray, ask, listen, and wait for His words to resonate inside of you. When we have His truth, we can distinguish when we need to take captive harmful thoughts.

Do not be conformed to this world, but be transformed by the renewal of your mind, that by testing you may discern what is the will of God, what is good and acceptable and perfect.

—Romans 12:2 ESV

We have authority through Christ Jesus to take the lies of the enemy and make them submit to the living Word of God.

Let's go to battle sister!

Example Battle Strategy

1. **The Lie**—It's messy. There is so much. Where do I even begin? Why bother? I am who I am, and it will always be this way. This is all there is for me.
2. **The Truth**—"*But now you have been set free from sin and have become slaves of God, the fruit you get leads to sanctification and its end, eternal life.*" (Romans 6:22 ESV)
3. **The Replacement**—That was who I once was, but my past was buried with Christ. I am new, I am whole, and He is doing a new thing in me! To God be the glory, He wastes nothing!
4. **The Declaration**—I declare that I am new in Him. God has set me free from past sins, from old ways of thinking, and has given me a new name. I receive this freedom. I proclaim that I am new in Christ and He has freedom for me. God, my story is yours—use it, my season, and my situation for your glory!

1. **The Lie**—How could someone possibly love and accept me? Better to keep my guard up and keep people out. They would just hurt and abandon me like everyone else.
2. **The Truth**—"'*For I know the plans I have for you,' declares the LORD, 'plans to prosper you and not to harm you, plans to give you hope and a future.*'" (Jeremiah 29:11 NIV)
3. **The Replacement**—I am loved, chosen by my heavenly Father, and designed for a purpose! I replace shame, guilt, and self-hate with love, grace, and celebration, because His Word never returns void. You see me, God. You know my every need and desire. I trust you.
4. **The Declaration**—I declare that I am worthy of love. I am known, loved, and seen by my heavenly Father. I proclaim freedom over my mind, and I break all chains of self-hate, guilt, shame, loneliness, and captivity in Christ Jesus. You, God will bring me to victory. Surround me! This moment, I rise above the lies, and thoughts, and I

rebuke you Satan, in Jesus' name. You have no place here. I am a daughter of the King, and His plans are to prosper me in my life, for good, for me! This the foundation I stand on!

Practical Fighting Tip: Be Prepared

Being aware of your surroundings is step one. Second is being prepared. A basic example of this—always walk to your car with your head up and keys in hand. Even more so, I was taught to walk with a key tucked in between my knuckles, key part facing out, so if someone did attack, one punch or hook would have more impact with a key to the face. If you are a gun carrier, that is a method of being prepared. If you are putting kids in the car, load them in on one side, and lock the other doors as you get them secured.

Does it take time? Yes. Does it sound ridiculous to some? Yes. But being prepared is never about people pleasing. Being prepared is about protection with the greatest chance of escape and survival. Is preparation worth it? Every time.

We can all identify seasons we wish we would have known then what we know now. In my own journey I can identify ways I entered the season unprepared, ignoring warning flags from the Holy Spirit, proceeding on. Most of those seasons came with wounds and deep learning lessons. There is wisdom in slowing down to assess preparation in every season.

Prayer

Lord, I submit my mind to You and put on the helmet of salvation. I give You my thoughts, fears, and dreams. I am sorry for the times that I have elevated these above You. Forgive me for the times that I have cowered and bowed to them and not to Your truth—Your word or the freedom I have because Jesus died for me. Today I claim Your truth! These lies no longer have power. I take back the authority I have in You over my mind. I take the lies in my mind [list them out], and I replace them with Your truth. As a daughter of the King, I will no longer fall prey to the enemy's attacks, schemes, and lies, but stand confidently and victoriously that the battle has been won. No spirit but the Holy Spirit is welcome here. I am new in Christ and through Romans 12, I am renewing my mind. Thank You for loving me, Lord, for pursuing me, and for Your promise of more for my life. I receive it. In Jesus' name, Amen.

Discussion Questions

1. Have you believed in lies that you have received as your truth? If so, how?

2. What are strongholds that you have built in your life, even with good intentions to protect or guard yourself?

3. Where and how does the enemy like to target you best? These could be considered trigger memories, emotions, or moments in your life.

4. What past event replays in your mind that you need to surrender to the Lord and ask Him to rewrite for you?

5. What new truth can you declare over your mind?

6
The Battle Against Our Words

"Death and life are in the power of the tongue, and those who love it will eat its fruits."
— Proverbs 18:21 (ESV)

If the battle originates in our minds, then I would say we confirm or enforce it with our words. according to Proverbs the impact of our words determines the outcome of our life- death of life. What we say either enforces what is in our minds or challenges and redirects what our minds are telling us. We have that ability; can you believe that? **Not everything our minds think has to come out of our mouths or be accepted as truth.**

Words are singularly the most powerful force available to humanity. We can choose to use this force constructively with words of encouragement, or destructively using words of despair. Words have energy and power with the ability to help, to heal, to hinder, to hurt, to harm, to humiliate and to humble.— Yehuda Berg, "The Power of Words"

Scientifically, it has been proven that it's easier to think and speak negatively than positively. The thoughts we have and the words we speak create patterns that shape our beliefs, which impact our actions, which direct our behavior. What we speak about ourselves and others, next to our thoughts, have the greatest impact on our lives. Our words have ripple effects, like rings of water...even into future generations!

Declarations for Victory in the Bible

Esther: *Go, assemble all the Jews who are found in Susa, and fast for me; do not eat or drink for three days, night or day. I and my maidens also will fast in the same way. And thus I will go in to the king, which is not according to the law; and if I perish, I perish.* — Esther 4:16 NASB

Jonah: *While I was fainting away, I remembered the LORD, and my prayer came to You, into Your holy temple. Those who regard vain idols forsake their faithfulness, but I will sacrifice to You with the voice of thanksgiving. That which I have vowed I will pay. Salvation is from the Lord.* — Jonah 2:7-9 NASB

Job: *I know that You can do all things, and that no plan is impossible for You. Who is this who conceals advice without knowledge? Therefore I have declared that which I did not understand, Things too wonderful for me, which I do not know. Please listen and I will speak; I will ask You, and You instruct me. I have heard of You by the hearing for the ear; but now my eye sees You; therefore I retract, and I repent, sitting on dust and ashes.* — Job 42:2-6 NASB

Joshua & Caleb: A*nd they spoke to all the congregation of the sons of Israel, saying, "The land which we passed through to spy out is an exceedingly good land. If the LORD is pleased with us, then He will bring us into this land and give it to us—a land which flows with milk and honey. Only do not rebel against the LORD; and do not fear the people of the land, for they will be our prey. Their protection is gone from them, and the LORD is with us; do not fear them."* — Numbers 14:7-9 NASB

David & Goliath- *The LORD who saved me from the paw of the lion and the paw of the bear, He will save me from the hand of this Philistine.* — 1 Samuel 17:37 NASB

Daniel: *My God, incline Your ear and hear! Open Your eyes and see our desolations and the city which is called by Your name; for we are not presenting our pleas before You based on any merits of our own, but based on Your great compassion. Lord, hear! Lord, forgive! Lord, listen and act! For Your own sake, my God, do not delay, because Your city and Your people are called by Your name.* — Daniel 9:18-19 NASB

Shadrach, Meshach & Abed-nego: *Shadrach, Meshach, and Abed-nego replied to the king, "Nebuchadnezzar, we are not in need of an answer to give you concerning this matter. If it be so, our God whom we serve is able to rescue us from the furnace of blazing fire; and He will rescue us from your hand, O king. But even if He does not, let it be known to you, O king, that we are not going to serve your gods nor worship the golden statue that you have set up."* — Daniel 3:16-18 NASB

I Can't

The day had come for my black belt test. I was a wreck with nerves. The test was broken out into various portions, starting, and ending the day with the most taxing physical portions. A few hours in, it was time to begin sparring. Fighting back the tears, I told my instructor, *"I can't keep going, I am so tired."* My instructor got in my face, locked eyes with mine, speaking with authority, "*Danielle, yes you can. This is what you have trained for. Do not give up now. Dig deep, get mad, and go out there. You can do this!"*

I don't know if it was his words, or the fact that I wasn't simply going to walk out, but I finished. I received my new belt and cried a few happy tears that it was done. There's a certain point of intersection between the mind and our words where the game can change.

Maybe you have encountered a season that you felt, "*I can't. I don't know how I will go on."* What we say gives power to something or someone in that season. When we label a season or event as "I can't" we are doing two things:

1. In our hopelessness, we give greater power and focus to the circumstance over the sovereignty and deep love of our Heavenly Father.

2. We look and sound just like the world.

I don't like pain, I really dislike pruning seasons, and I have a hard time when I am not in control. No one shows up happy to closed doors, heartbreaking news, broken promises, or seasons of failure and loneliness. **It's what we do with those moments, and how we navigate those seasons differently than the world that makes our testimony stand out for Him.** Our mindset is internal, our words are external. Our words show others a lot about what we really believe to be true about our Jesus and His power.

Just because we think something doesn't make it true. We have far more in us than we realize, and if we are honest, we have probably disqualified ourselves or walked away from several of the right fights because we were tired. We can do this. We can do hard things because our God has the final word. He is at work, even in this.

The Sword of the Spirit

In chapter 3 we talked about the armor of God. Remember, the sword of the Spirit is our weapon. The sword is God's Word. In the simplest form, the Bible is God's love letter to us, His sons and daughters. His Word is filled with wisdom, stories from generations past of trials and triumph, encouragement, and caution. Through His Word and the gift of the Holy Spirit, we get to know His heart, His character, and His deep love for us individually.

When we allow His words and His truth to be our weapon, it silences the enemy. Not our words, His. Going through the words of those in the Bible during moments of deep testing and trust, I was both strengthened and encouraged how they chose to use their words to take a stand. Their words delivered complete clarity in line with God's will to protect, defend, and bless what God had called them to. In every story, there is victory. When God speaks, our best posture is immediate obedience. His Word, His guidance will yield a victory beyond natural understanding or belief every time.

Surviving

Growing up, my mom would often use the phrase "we were just surviving." Coming from a divorced home with three other siblings, two of whom were very sick children, my mother's own sickness went undetected. I can only imagine my grandmother, an unbeliever at the time, constantly living in a state of survival: for her babies, for her marriage, for herself. Through the years, I saw that my grandmother carried around a fractured view of herself, her value, and her worth. She was bitter. The limited information I know of my great-grandmother, her mother, is that she was not a kind, loving, or nurturing mother to her daughter. Hurt people, hurt people.

Circumstantially, both my grandmother and my mother have walked very different roads and endured a lot of tough things that warranted "seasons of surviving." However, I noticed this phrase popping up in my own life when things got hard, contained uncertainty, or seemed unfair. With all grace, empathy and good intentions, my mother would tell me, "you are just surviving." It began to feel like a cycle—a tough season in life would arise, something that externally seemed hard or unfair. I began to label hard seasons and poor choices with the response that I was "just surviving."

While I excused myself in my words and thinking, I wasn't comforted or proud of them. I realized that how I personally was giving myself grace, I was using it as an excuse for escape. A few years back, I attended a women's retreat, where we unpacked generational patterns— actions or beliefs that have been carried from one generation to the next. This phrase and cycle of "just surviving" came to mind. I began to wonder if the "survival season" and belief was much bigger than I had realized. Through prayer, I began to inquire if this simple phrase was a limiting tactic from the enemy for previous generations. Memories of several seasons and experiences flashed through my mind. Things that were painful, that I wasn't proud of, encounters I really believed disqualified me from a life I truly wanted.

With prayer and asking that simple question, a fresh perspective entered: If I take my season and circumstances, the very ones that God claims to be in, the very seasons in which I believe God has gone before me and is working all things together for good (Romans 8:28), then I have a choice.

Using my words, I began to change the narrative of past hurt seasons and circumstances. I began to see differently—no longer would I allow the hurts to dominate the narrative, but rather celebrate the growth that came out of those seasons and what God's grace was doing in me. Surviving implied me as the victim. I painted that narrative with my own words in how I shared my story. But I wasn't a victim, nor did I ever want to be. However, each time I would share my story or a season that had hurt, I was speaking that narrative, affirming that belief over my life.

With that new God-given lens, I began to declare both internally and externally that I was a victor, not a victim. I was an overcomer, not just a survivor. My season built me; it didn't bury me. I wrote out that my life would be a testimony of His goodness, His faithfulness, and that through all my shortcomings and limitations, my life would be for His glory.

As small and innocent as that phrase may seem to you, it helped me to discover a pattern beginning. Previously, and often unintentionally, I would give power to the circumstance that I was in by assigning blame with excuses, but I didn't like how my life looked or how I felt. If God is always at work, refining and perfecting us more into His likeness, then I don't want to allow myself or my family to "survive." We run the risk of allowing our life and circumstances to define our value, victory, and story

The pattern of allowing limiting beliefs and phrases when things were hard had to end. For years, I had been waiting for my life to get better. I would often say "when this happens, then I will be______." I began to wonder, "what if I allow this season or this thing to become my whole story, more than a chapter in my book? What if I miss out on what God has for me, even in these dark, lonely places?" A tiny, simple, and seemingly innocent phrase—a mentality that I can trace back at least two generations—held power in my life. Unbroken, it affected my thoughts, my behavior, and subtly everything I did. Remember, out of the overflow of the heart… the mouth speaks.

Watch your thoughts, they become words;
watch your words, they become actions;
watch your actions, they become habits;

watch your habits, they become character;
watch your character, for it becomes your destiny.
— Frank Outlaw

If I didn't change my view or my words in those trying seasons, I was potentially at risk of "surviving" my whole life. Determined to live a life I loved of freedom, joy, and wholeness, I decided to stop owning that phrase as the banner over my mind. I began leaning in to what was happening and why it was happening, and more importantly what Scripture had to say about all of it. Let me tell you, the game changed.

Our words carry more power than we know. Our words impact more aspects of our lives than we realize, because they are tied to beliefs in our hearts. Our words are the side effects surfacing from the roots inside.

What Do You Say about Yourself?

We are our own worst critics. What is the internal dialogue you speak regarding the season you're in? What is the story you repeat regarding **that** mistake you made? What do you say about those goals and dreams you have or had?

We are the only ones who will ever know all the things that we tell ourselves, which is comforting and dangerous at the same time. If we speak toxic, shaming, and degrading things towards ourselves, then we are establishing ourselves as women prone to crumble under the pressure of anyone and anything. I trust myself more than I trust anyone else, so if I am telling myself terrible things about me, then I will hold onto that as my truth.

Think about this with me: If I heard a friend speaking this way about herself, the very things I say about myself, what would I say to her? What would I think? You would be shocked at what she was saying, pondering how she could possibly see or believe those things about herself.

"I could never do that."
"I don't deserve that. This is what I deserve."
"I'm fat."
"I wish I was special to someone."
"I wish I had what she has."
"This always happens to me. Why me?!"
"I'm so ugly. I wish I was pretty like her."
"I always fail. Why try?"

God's Word doesn't say any of these things over us. These are lies from the enemy. When we speak these over our lives, we are inviting the enemy to have residence in our lives. God speaks life over our seasons and the future ahead with hope and truth! We have to choose, every day, all day, to know those truths and speak them over our lives, especially when the lies invade.

*Set a guard, O LORD, over my mouth; keep watch over the door of my lip*s.
— Psalm 141:3 ESV

The words we speak are one of the greatest aspects that set us apart as those that have wisdom and biblical fools. There are over fifty-four Scriptures regarding the tongue and the words we speak! Here are just a few:

> *Sin is not ended by multiplying words, but the prudent hold their tongues.* — Proverbs 10:19 NIV

> *A gentle answer turns away wrath, but a harsh word stirs up anger.*
> — Proverbs 15:1 NIV

> *With the fruit of a man's mouth his stomach will be satisfied; He will be satisfied with the product of his lips. Death and life are in the power of the tongue, and those who love it will eat its fruit.*
> — Proverbs 18:20-21 NASB

Set a guard, O LORD, over my mouth; keep watch over the door of my lips. — Psalm 141:3 NASB

The one who guards his mouth preserves his life; the one who opens wide his lips comes to ruin. — Proverbs 13:3 NASB

He who guards his mouth and his tongue, guards his soul from troubles. — Proverbs 21:23 NASB

The one who desires life, to love and see good days, must keep his tongue from evil and his lips from speaking deceit. He must turn away from evil and do good; he must seek peace and pursue it. — 1 Peter 3:10-11 NASB

Let your speech always be with grace, as though seasoned with salt, so that you will know how you should respond to each person. — Colossians 4:6 NASB

Let no unwholesome word proceed from your mouth, but only such a word as is good for edification according to the need of the moment, so that it will give grace to those who hear. Do not grieve the Holy Spirit of God, by whom you were sealed for the day of redemption. — Ephesians 4:29-30 NASB

When there are many words, transgression is unavoidable, but he who restrains his lips is wise. — Proverbs 10:19 NASB

Let the words of my mouth and the meditation of my heart be acceptable in Your sight, O LORD, my strength and my Redeemer. — Psalm 19:14 NKJV

It is not what enters into the mouth that defiles the man, but what proceeds out of the mouth, this defiles the man. — Matthew 15:11 NASB

Kids + Words

Fighting For Freedom

Wise words are like deep waters; wisdom flows from the wise like a bubbling brook. — Proverbs 18:4 NLT

Don't skip over this part even if you do not have kids. I was that type of reader—if it didn't apply to me, I didn't read it. This part is just as much for you, regardless of whether you are a mom, or friends with a woman that is. Through my own life and now as a mom of four, I want to encourage a deeper look into the words we speak to, around, and about children. Our words lay a foundation for tomorrow, the day after that, and so forth.

There are common sayings that have innocent intention, but we have adapted them as normal, side-stepping opportunities where we could speak life. Changing the narrative looks like:

> "Terrible twos" becomes "terrific twos"—not because it's easy, not because you are trying to impress anyone, but because a child is only two once. In that year there will be sweet gifts, alongside hard times that sets the foundation for age three. What kind of year do we want to have with our kids? How do we want our children to grow up hearing about the age and stage as a two-year-old? What might we be missing out on because we have labeled both the season and the child?
>
> "Wild child" becomes "passionate and determined."
> "Head in the clouds" becomes "big dreams and incredible vision."
> "Stubborn" becomes "focused and persistent."
> "Rebellious" becomes "trailblazer pursuing their own path."

The first statements may be true. If you have spent time with children, you have probably seen that we don't need to teach sin. We are all born with it. The role of parents is to guide these littles to use their God-given characteristics away from sin in a constructive manner that will bring glory to the kingdom one day.

If we put bits into the mouths of horses so that they obey us, we guide their whole bodies as well. Look at the ships also: though they are so large and are driven by strong winds, they are guided by a very small rudder wherever the will of the pilot directs. — James 3:3-4 ESV

Words and phrases are small things but think about a rudder on the ship. If the captain changes the rudder ever so slightly, the direction of the ship changes drastically over time. A small change is usually unnoticed, but over time is undeniable.

As parents and friends of parents, choosing words that are rooted in truth, and potential to see past the moment, is a choice. Life-giving words give life and are a positive fight for kids and their future. I wish someone had done that for me—both in my childhood and early teenage years. A simple change in narrative, a deep belief in the work God was doing would have changed a lot for me. Words spoken over me at fifteen had deep and painful holds on me until I was thirty-one. Let's not allow another generation to carry forth what we are working to break free from now.

I AM Statements

One of the most powerful things we can do is begin to declare our truth in bold statements! Declarations highlight the strengths within us, the belief of things that we may not see or believe yet. Let's be bold together and build some "I AM" declarations. This might be uncomfortable. We tend to do a terrible job celebrating our own God-given gifts, but this is our time to own it and proclaim it.

These statements can be simple: I AM strong. I AM beautiful. I AM chosen. I AM known fully and loved by God. I AM an overcomer. I AM strong. I AM worth love. Two words and everything else that follows is up to you and how the Lord leads!

I AM…

Below are a few examples of a few of my own **I AM** statements:

> **I AM** worthy of love. I have value, and my story has a purpose for the kingdom.
> **I AM** a woman who waives a flag of victory so others know their story can too.
> **I AM** courageous, passionate, and bold. I am unashamedly taking new territory for the Lord.
> **I AM** an encourager and a champion of women. I have been positioned to call out the gifts and strengths in other women.

Those were hard to write at first. In fact, I needed help from others to share what they saw in me. Even when I tried to think of writing things down, a voice would enter my head— "How in the world would you do that? Why do you think you could accomplish that? You don't have this, this, and this, like she did, so you would never be able to do that." That was the enemy talking. It wouldn't let up until the thoughts stopped. In the past, it seemed like a dance would begin, the steps went something like this:

1. Hope
2. The lying voice in my head
3. My response: "Oh gosh, yep, so true, ok, well never mind then."
4. The lying voice: "Ha, what a silly thought! Let's watch an episode of *Friends.*"
5. I turned on the desired episode, and that was the end of it.

That was the problem, not me. The cycle would happen, and instead of standing up to fight for myself, or the gifts and passions God had placed inside, I backed down and allowed lies to lead because I doubted my worth.

It is not what enters into the mouth that defiles the man, but what proceeds out of the mouth, this defiles the man. — Matthew 15:11 NASB

I want you to write your **I AM** statements. Repeat them to yourself, post them on the bathroom mirror, keep them in your car, put them anywhere that you can see them to remind yourself to declare truth over lies. These statements have helped countless women draw out truth when their thoughts and words were being targeted by the enemy.

Declaring **I AM** statements with authority stirs a few things:

1. The power in our words begins to break strategic lies from the enemy and weave strength, truth, and hope through our very beings.

2. The more we obediently own our words and gifts for the Lord, the stronger our weapon against the enemy becomes.

If you don't know your gifts, strengths, or dreams, let's take a moment and discover some amazing things about yourself together through these questions!

What were the dreams, hobbies, or interests that you had growing up? Why?

What is a topic that fascinates you—something you could spend all day reading, writing, or talking about?

What has been one of the biggest defining seasons in your story?

If money was of no value, what would you do?

Is there a recurring thought that the Lord has continued to prompt you with?

What is the lie you hear when you begin to think or dream about the future?

If you still have questions, head over to DanielleWingate.com and message me. I want you to help you see purpose, and to find hope and freedom in your story.

There is no judgement. You don't even have to share this with anyone, although I would encourage finding a friend to do this with. It's important that you give yourself a safe place to dream and to write out these things. Please fight for yourself to pray, dream, and write free from al shame and limitations. It's time to celebrate and soak in the fullness of who God has created you to be. It's important that we own our stories for His glory; there is power in our testimony. Once we begin celebrating ourselves and how we have been created, it is much easier to celebrate victories, and the differences and strengths of others, because we can appreciate how God is working in them too. Our lives are not a competition. Every story matters. Every person is valuable!

Example Battle Strategy

1. **The Lie** — I am the way I am. I can't change.
2. **The Truth** —Through Christ, you can "put off your old self" and renew your thoughts and attitudes (Ephesians 4:22-24).
3. **The Replacement** — I replace the lie that in Christ, I am a new creation. The old has gone, and the new has come (2 Corinthians 5:17).
4. **The Declaration** — In Jesus' name, I speak against the lie that I am unable to change, and I speak to the mindset to protect myself from the vulnerability that it takes to change. God has made me a new creation in Him. He is redeeming my story. No longer will this phrase limit me from becoming all that Christ has called me to be. I surrender it today. I lay it at the foot of the cross, and I submit fully and wholly into the new work that God is doing in me!

1. **The Lie**—It doesn't matter what I said if I was right, and they deserved it.
2. **The Truth**—The world may see it that way, but my call is greater. Let my words be seasoned with grace, so that it is pleasing to God (Ephesians 4:29-30).
3. **The Replacement**—Today I replace the statement and belief that what comes out of my mouth is justified, depending on the actions of someone else with the truth that sin is only multiplied when I respond poorly (Proverbs 10:19). I embrace a new statement that my words will be life-giving to all, seasoned with grace, because I have been given grace.
4. **The Declaration**—I take authority and ownership over my words and my beliefs towards others. Lord, I choose to surrender negative and justified thought patterns and to release another's action over to You. Help my words to be kind, seasoned with grace, and to be life-giving to all who hear. I rebuke you, Satan. Your presence in me ends now, my words and my calling belong to the Lord! Jesus, bless the person today and forgive me in what I have said to or about them.

Practical Fighting Tip: Deflect Energy

There are various forms of martial arts. Judo is style designed around using the opponent's force against themselves. This style has fascinated me, as one of the least aggressive, primarily focused on the opponents' actions and efforts on the ground, coordinating how to use their force to your advantage with patient persistence. Contrary to what many of us think of when it comes to fighting. It's methodical, soft, and patient. As the attacks come for us, we can discern and deflect the attacks as we pursue in prayer how to navigate the battle.

Prayer

Jesus, I am sorry for the ways I have misused my words about myself and others. I realize the power in the words that I speak, and I desire to use my words for Your glory, to uplift others, and to speak life over myself. Forgive me Father, I take full responsibility for my actions, and I receive Your forgiveness. I claim that You are making me new, even now. I don't need to do or be anything more than present, in this moment, in relationship with You.

I rebuke the attacks of the enemy, in Jesus' name! I bind them up and send them to the pit of Hell. I replace the lies [speak them out] with Your truth, that I am [fill in from your **I AM** statements]. I claim the victory, freedom, and truth that is already promised to me, knowing that this battle has been won through You. Thank You for loving me. Thank You for seeing me, renewing me, and pursuing me.

Discussion Questions

1. What phrases or labels have you noticed that you or your family have said repetitively?

2. Referencing Frank Outlaw's quote, is there an experience that you can trace your actions back to because of your words and thoughts? If so, what was it?

3. If a friend heard you speaking about yourself, what would she say to you?

4. Who are one or two people that you can share your **I AM** statements with to help you change your narrative?

5. What lie has been exposed with your words that you need to break free from and replace with truth?

7
The Battle Against Our Past

If you don't heal what hurt you, you'll bleed on people who didn't cut you.
—Unknown

What's on the Inside Comes Out

Bitterness and anger had become good friends of mine. Choices from a family member, empty promises, and actions created a roller coaster effect for all involved. On three different occasions I pursued counseling for resolution, mostly because I was afraid of what the hurt was doing to me. Grace and forgiveness seemed like far-off realities. The minute I took a step forward, Satan was quick to remind me, "Danielle, you have every right to be angry." For a long time, I took a step forward and two steps back. Two steps forward, one step back. I worked hard to get over it, get past it, but try as I might, I continued to return to similar behaviors, emotions, and thoughts. Whatever is on the inside will come out. I promise you that. Through counseling and deep internal digging, I began to see how the "flare ups" of bitterness, unforgiveness, hurt, and anger were manifesting in other ways, keeping me bound to the same condition I had been in:

> **Dating**—When I engaged in a romantic sort of relationship and things didn't go as "desired or planned," I responded irrationally. I allowed the offense to take root in my heart, being sure to remind the boyfriend of his "sin" against me. Somehow, I believed if I kept the offense or the past hurt in front of me, I wouldn't be blindsided by a future one. Secretly, I hoped I was protecting myself against more hurt. Anger lurked below the surface. When a miscommunication transpired, we would go from 0 to 60 instantly. The poor guy was so confused, "Danielle, where is this coming from? How in the world do I fix this?" Life was an emotional roller coaster.

Professionally—The ability to receive feedback well is essential to success. However, when you see and hear things through a lens of bitterness, hurt, and anger, it cripples a healthy lens to effectively receive. At an annual review my boss gave me some good guidance and expressed some well-needed critique and concerns regarding communication with fellow leaders. At the time, I didn't see any of this as accurate. Caught off guard and deeply offended, I countered, "Jerry! How could you say that after how hard I have worked, after all the effort I have made to establish this venture? They are…," and the blaming and complaining began. Moments later, tears began to fall. Bewilderment came over his face. Calmly and professionally, he excused me from the table to go "collect myself" in the restroom and return when I was ready. Angrily storming off, I paced in the bathroom, vented silently, and cried heavily. Truth be told, I contemplated quitting and walking out that day, thinking "I'll show them!" My boss patiently and kindly invested in me, yet strategically, continued to challenge me to grow. Looking back, I had similar encounters at a few other places of work; it was me, not them.

Personally—Anger manifested the worst with my immediate family. When solutions and answers didn't seem possible, I shut down emotionally, lashing out when the frustration and pain grew too great on the inside. From money to quality time, to emotional encouragement, to physical support, to spiritual interceding—I shielded them from all of it. I thought, "I have been hurt. The promises have been broken. I am not going to fall for this again." I refused any sort of help to avoid any vulnerability. My thought process was, "No more access = No more hurting."

I became great at crossing my arms, pointing the finger, and making excuses. The problem is that mentality and those actions only entangled and trapped me in a life I didn't want to be in. Bitterness, hurt, and regret don't hurt the other person, they poison the one holding on to them by stealing their joy, clarity of mind, and eliminating the possibility for peace and growth. Forgetting and moving on with my life wasn't the answer either, although I tried that. Memories, seasons, and lessons are part of our stories. What matters is whose truth we are listening to about those past seasons, God's truth or Satan's lies?

It Didn't Bury You—It Built You

We express varying degrees of confidence in our memories. Our brains are wired to piece together events and feelings to create seamless narratives. Each time we recall a memory, we recall the most prominent details altering our stories.

In the battle against our past, Satan uses people, memories, scents, and experiences or situations that made us believe we were unworthy, unqualified, and unloved. As the king of deception, he spins lies that seem like truth in our current season, relevant to what we are walking now with those old comfortable feelings that "fit" right in. This is the tension to be vigilantly focused on God's truth and His promises, in which we choose to expose those lies or memories to the light of God's Word and replace them with His truth, taking authority over them. This may mean daily, sometimes hourly. Don't be fooled; the enemy will stop at nothing to get you to doubt and question God's Word.

How we overcome experiences and pitfalls in the past are some of the greatest defining elements of who we are and who we are becoming. We aren't children with split homes. We are not the ones who never fit in, the ones who never made it, the ones who were cheated on, the divorced ones. Those are experiences, not identities. We should allow these events to build us and shape us, but not define us.

I wish there was some pretty answer as to why things happen, or some promise that one day we would understand, but there isn't. What I can tell you is that the Bible promises trials will come (John 16:33).

Consider it pure joy, my brothers and sisters, whenever you face trials of many kinds, because you know that the testing of your faith produces perseverance. Let perseverance finish its work so that you may be mature and complete, not lacking anything. —James 1:2-4 NIV®

God also promises to overcome with victory. You are still living and breathing. Those hard things didn't take you out; you are still here, being refined and pruned, being positioned for all that He has for you!

Satan wants to use past hurts and offenses to give permission for bitterness and hurt to dwell and disqualify us. **When we allow hurts of our past to rule over us, we allow the lies of the enemy to reside within us.** The father of lies, the king of deception, wants nothing more than a place to establish and grow in our lives to imprison us and distance us from relationship with the Father. All he needs is access, a foothold in.

"In your anger do not sin": Do not let the sun go down while you are still angry, and do not give the devil a foothold. — Ephesians 4:26-27 NIV®

I don't know what you have walked; I don't know who has hurt you or the pain that you carry. If no one has said it before, let me tell you this:

> **I am sorry for the pain and hurt that you have encountered, for the people that have let you down when they should have been there. I'm sorry for the experiences outside of your control that you had to navigate. I'm sorry for the offenses of other hurt and broken people. It wasn't fair, it wasn't right, it doesn't make it ok.**

In some ways I wish I could shield you from your pain and wipe the memories of those seasons away. On the other hand, I want to ask some questions: What if everything in your past was to build you? What if God allowed it to grow you, and to equip you for this season? And the next one, and the one after that? What if God allowed you to experience your situation, so you could show others how to rise above and fight through it? All we see is past and present, but we have no idea the capacity in which God wants to use us going forward.

Satan is working against us just enough so that we return to the hurt and find comfort in the familiar. Let's be honest, sometimes, or oftentimes where we have been is more comfortable than a new unknown. Meanwhile, God is at work, inviting us to press on and press into Him, encouraging us to rise above and persevere. He has given us His Holy Spirit as our advocate to tell us exactly what He longs for us to know, the next step. Sometimes, the word is to remain and abide. Sometimes, it's to take a courageous step forward. Sometimes, it's to stop and rest. The important thing is that we press into Him daily and label His truths all over our past.

Forgiveness

To navigate this battle, we need to be obedient to His Word and address one thing first—forgiveness.

If you are where I have been, then you probably just cringed reading that word. It's ok, you are in good company. We are going to do this together, because your calling is too big and the risk is too great to leave unattended.

Forgive: to stop feeling angry or resentful towards someone for an offense, flaw, or mistake

Forgiveness is a release—an internal change to keep us from being imprisoned. It does nothing for the other person. Hypothetically speaking, forgiveness is 90% about us and 10% about the offender. This process is about protection from the enemy—protection against our feelings, mindset, heart, and purpose. Remember, no points of entry for him to rule from!

I used to think that forgiving someone meant giving them permission to continue the hurt or forgetting about it, but it's not. Every situation is different, and we should evaluate each one and draw healthy boundaries as such, but the need for forgiveness doesn't change. This is about us, not them, and it's never a question of whether they deserve it or not. Forgiveness is essential to true freedom.

Sin separates us from God, period. As believers, we should strive to grow in righteousness daily, God's right way of living. **Someone's offenses towards us—that's their sin. They will be held accountable one day for that; how we respond to their sin is where our sin comes into play.** We will be accountable for what we say and how we respond.

If we confess our sins, he is faithful and just to forgive us our sins and to cleanse us from all unrighteousness.—1 John 1:9 ESV

I continue to pray against frustration and work to continue forgiving. For me, in the big situations with those closest, it's not a one and done thing. Maybe sometimes, but not usually for me.

I'm going to ask you to do something big with me. If you have never prayed a prayer to forgive the other person or experience, I want to do that with you now. This doesn't excuse or approve the action. This choice is to bring healing to you, evict Satan from cohabitating in your mind, and take your freedom back. If you don't "feel" ready, ask God to help you. If the tears start to come, that's okay. This isn't easy. It's ridiculously hard, but we are going after freedom here. We are taking territory back from the enemy. Would you expect it any other way? This is hard, but you can do hard things!

Pray this with me:

Dear Jesus, You know the hurt I have walked. I don't want to carry the pain of the past. I trust You. I trust that You were there with me then, You are here with me now, and You have already gone before me. Lord, I don't want any part of me bound, closed off, or restrained to what You have for my life. Pour out Your abundance, God. I want Your freedom, Your joy, and above all, Your peace. Through You, God, I forgive [say the name or situation]. *This is no longer mine to carry, but I give it to You, fully releasing the hurt and bitterness. God, give me a renewed heart, a renewed mind, and a renewed spirit. Thank You for Your faithfulness. I praise You that my story is not done, and that You have never left me. I break the chains of the past, replacing them with Your truth and the hope of the promise from You for a future. You are making all things new, I claim that today. In Jesus' name, amen.*

Breathe in. Breathe out. Congratulations—you have just taken a huge brave step! A step towards your freedom and healing. Satan hates what you have just done. Keep it up.

A Deeper Look

While our past is our past, it consists of connections, emotions, and encounters with other imperfect, broken people. That is known. What is unknown is the other things that may be limiting us, things that we need to take authority over and specifically pray through as the Lord reveals them. When it comes to our freedom, we don't want anything lingering. Let's talk about what three of these unknowns could be: strongholds, word curses, and generational patterns.

1. **Strongholds**

   The Merriam-Webster dictionary defines a *stronghold* as a place that has been fortified to protect against an attack. The Hebrew translation of stronghold is *metsad* — a place with limited or difficult access or a fortress. The NASB references this word and definition eleven times in the Bible.

   A stronghold is something you have unknowingly built—a tower or fortress to protect yourself against opposing threats. Sounds reasonable. Maybe you have built fortresses to protect yourself from things like shame, rejection, passivity, control, and self-hatred. Amidst our good intentions against external threats, we can become trapped and bound in our own fortresses, giving Satan a place to lead from.

   Listen, this may sound like a lot, but stick with me. I knew I had wounds from stuff with my family, right? Going through an intentional study on freedom, my eyes were opened when I realized I had built strongholds. The tallest, most established stronghold in my life was formed on a foundation of rejection.

Here are a few examples of where rejection can grow from:

- Absentee fathers or mothers
- Lack of bonding with parents
- Parents' divorce
- Not being "wanted"
- Various forms of abuse—verbal, physical, sexual
- Parents' addictions
- Constant fighting or strife
- Unjust discipline
- Competition with siblings

Here are examples of some of the fruit that the stronghold of rejection can produce:

- Reliance on personal coping mechanisms, instead of the truth from God
- Rebellion—aggressive attitudes, stubbornness, defiance, fighting, etc.
- Pride and arrogance
- Control and manipulation
- Harshness, skepticism, and unbelief
- Fear, anxiety, worry, negativity, and pessimism
- Performance-based life, relationships, and ministry
- Overachievement, competition, and perfectionism
- Withdrawal, isolation, and independence

Reading through my stories, you might have noticed that the last three were the very "fruit" that my stronghold of rejection drove. They gripped me to my core. I realized that if I wanted freedom, I was going to have to work to break down my fortress and break free from my stronghold of rejection. With that discovery, I was able to identify the control center for the enemy's leading point in my life, and with God's help, I knew my target to demolish.

2. **Generational Patterns**

Regardless of the family we grew up in, we have inherited a culture—mannerisms, sayings, and beliefs. Positive and negative aspects are passed down through generations as we see in 2 Timothy 1:5 (NIV), "*I am reminded of your sincere faith, which first lived in your grandmother Lois and in your mother Eunice and, I am persuaded, now lives in you also.*" One way to begin to identify generational patterns are the stories and details that we notice being passed down through the generations.

My great-grandmother desired a closer relationship with her mother. Out of her own hurt, she withheld from her daughters, who withheld from their daughters, igniting a feeling of rejection. The situations and circumstances were different, the people changed, but I found myself beginning to hold to a similar mindset.

And he passed in front of Moses, proclaiming, "The LORD, the LORD, the compassionate and gracious God, slow to anger, abounding in love and faithfulness, maintaining love to thousands, and forgiving wickedness, rebellion and sin. Yet he does not leave the guilty unpunished; he punishes the children and their children for the sin of the parents to the third and fourth generation.—Exodus 34:6-7 NIV

Pray and ask the Lord to reveal anything in your family line that not of Him. There is no reason or excuse to passively "accept" what has always been done or said in your family. This is a pursuit for your freedom. Here we take a stand to elevate God's truth over family culture and patterns. Bondage ends here. You ae taking a stand to change every generation after you.

You shall not bow down to them or serve them, for I the Lord your God am a jealous God, visiting the iniquity of the fathers on the children to the third and the fourth generation of those who hate me, but showing steadfast love to thousands of those who love me and keep my commandments.—Exodus 20:5-6 ESV

You must not bow down to them or worship them, for I, the LORD your God, am a jealous God who will not tolerate your affection for any other gods. I lay the sins of the parents upon their children; the entire family is affected—even children in the third and fourth generations of those who reject me. But I lavish unfailing love for a thousand generations on those who love me and obey my commands.—Deuteronomy 5:9-10 NLT

3. **Word Curses**

Simply put, these verbal occurrences are the opposite of verbal blessings. If we aren't aware of what is happening, we unknowingly receive word curses or offenses from other imperfect, broken people as our truth, a label that we can begin to carry. Through the person's opinion, and our reception of the words, we give access to the enemy. We have all encountered people who have expressed negative opinions regarding us. I encourage you to pray intentionally and ask God to show you if there is a label, nickname, mindset, or belief that you have adopted as your truth unknowingly.

Maybe you heard someone say things like, "You are dumb. You aren't pretty. If you could only be like this other person."

Like a fluttering sparrow or a darting swallow, an undeserved curse does not come to rest.—Proverbs 26:2 NIV

When we find ourselves thinking about these lies and labels, it's a flag for us to act against the attacks of the enemy. Word curses are another tactic against our past to shame us, bind us, and limit our effectiveness for the Kingdom.

We cannot take this lightly. If we want freedom from our past, we need to do some deep cleaning. The important thing is that we ask the Holy Spirit to reveal whatever it is. The second thing is that the pattern ends today. We don't have to pass it on to our kids, or their kids, or even carry it another day. With God's help and authority in Christ, we can address it, ask forgiveness for the past things of our family, and break that tie now. We will do this together at the end of the chapter.

The Lord is slow to anger and abounding in steadfast love, forgiving iniquity and transgression, but he will by no means clear the guilty, visiting the iniquity of the fathers on the children, to the third and the fourth generation.—Numbers 14:18 ESV

Roots, Not Symptoms

My sophomore year of high school was one of the hardest emotionally. After some poor choices with a boy, women who worked in the Christian school chose to share their opinions with me about my poor choices. In detail one shared her opinions of shame, disappointment, and embarrassment. I was fifteen. Almost twenty years later, I realized there were still parts of her words from that hallway experience that I had been carrying around.

Unknowingly, I permitted her words to take root and grow deep. Roots that reminded me often how I didn't measure up. Roots that echoed the message of disappointment and shame. I realize now that those were all lies from the enemy, and they were baggage that I carried, words I accepted which became beliefs that crippled me every step forward I tried to take. Beliefs became titles I allowed to contain me and words I allowed to chain me. That's just what the enemy wanted though. In the process of hearing and accepting the lies, I grew distant from God. Over time, I forgot how to get back to His truth for peace, hope, and guidance. For years I treaded water, trying to outwork the pain or simply create something new.

Satan wants us to hear the subtle words of others and allow them to take root. Our enemy wants those titles and affiliations we have been given to remind us why we aren't good enough, why we can't do something, and why we are unworthy. Why? **Lies from the enemy will always keep us from becoming the person we were fully called and created to be.** Those truths can only be found in God's Word and in relationship with Him. Lies from the enemy distort God's truth, limiting the impact we have if we remain chained by the words, opinions, and beliefs of anyone other than our heavenly Father. We all have sin, every single one of us, but God doesn't condemn us. He loves us and tells us, *"He has removed our sins as far as the east is from the west"* (Psalm 103:12 NLT).

Friend, if you are walking around today, carrying hurtful and harmful words that someone else spoke over you, ask God to redeem both those words and those memories. If you are unsure, ask God to expose the root of those emotions and thoughts where the enemy gained access into your life.

Here's what this looked like for me:

God, thank You for showing me the root of these lies. Lies that I am "not enough" or "unworthy," that I have to prove myself to others, [fill in your own, those were mine]. *I had no idea the power of the words. Maybe those women didn't know what they were truly saying either, but I forgive them. Today, I no longer allow those memories and their words to have a place in my life. Redeem those moments. Wash over every aspect of the memories with grace, with truth, and with love, like only You can. Heal those memories with a fresh perspective, so I can find purpose, and not only pain. I rebuke these lies from the enemy. I command them to be broken in Jesus' name, and I claim Your freedom. In You, Jesus, I claim health and restoration. You are making me new. Thank You for loving me, for seeing past all my flaws, and for relentlessly pursuing me. You are refining me to reflect You, to be more like You, and in that growth, I fall more in love with You. Bless those women, Father! Use this for Your glory!*

Grace

It's easy to speak clearly and confidently to the grace of the past, "look what God has done." As believers, we know the Word tells us that God will never leave us. So, we can also speak confidently regarding future grace for things, but rarely do we comprehend and extend present grace to ourselves. Maybe we forget that His grace is sufficient for us or that we don't have to be or do anything else for His love.

I *have been crucified with Christ; and it is no longer I who live, but Christ lives in me; and the life which I now live in the flesh I live by faith in the Son of God, who loved me and gave Himself up for me. I do not nullify the grace of God, for if righteousness comes through the Law, then Christ died needlessly.* —Galatians 2:20-22 NASB

This is important to grasp because the excuses will grow for why we can't access freedom. But God's Word is clear on this—His love and grace for us is enough. We must accept it and keep that gift, the truth of His endless grace forefront. Operating from a state of present grace changes everything from the inside out.

Example Battle Strategy

1. **The Lie**—There's no way God or anyone else can forgive me.
2. **The Truth**—Nothing can separate me from the love that you have for me, God (Romans 8:37-39). I am new in Christ, and He has reconciled Himself to me (2 Corinthians 5:17-18).
3. **The Replacement**—You are doing a new thing, Lord! I replace the lie with Your truth, I accept Your grace, and I forgive myself. You want to use me, and You promise to waste nothing (Isaiah 43:18-19).
4. **The Declaration**—I break ties with shame, with guilt, and with unforgiveness. Today, I am new in Christ, I am free, and God is doing something in me. God will redeem this.

1. **The Lie**—I need to keep my walls up. I must protect myself so people can't hurt me again.
2. **The Truth**—Through weakness you are made great. I can stand confidently and share courageously for you will be glorified (2 Corinthians 12:9-10).
3. **The Replacement**—Help me, Lord, to no longer carry pride for protection, but to replace that lie and draw near to You as Your Word says that You will then draw near to me. In Your time, You will lift me up to honor (James 4:1-10).
4. **The Declaration**—Today, I choose to both forgive [insert person(s) name(s)] and bless them. I take my authority back and I give it You, God. May You use even this. Today healing begins, today old walls are being broken down, and I proclaim victory and honor in Your time, God. To You be the glory, have Your way, Lord.

Practical Fighting Tip: Strike with Purpose

As we have talked previously, our best action is always to escape or leave an attack. But if you cannot, strike with purpose. This doesn't mean a light slap or a push. Every second counts. An attacker needs to know that you are both prepared and intent on not becoming the victim. We never start the fight, we don't encourage it; it is 100 percent self-defense. If you do need to make contact through hitting or kicking an opponent, do so with the intent to get distance so you can get away and find help. Practical areas to make contact are the nose, the throat, or the ears.

The enemy loves to use our past to disqualify us and shame us. Striking with purpose looks like stopping the lies as soon as they begin, putting them in their place, ensuring the enemy knows that you will not be made a victim to your past. Not today, not ever.

Prayer

Lord, You are holy. Thank You for this new revelation. You are showing me a new path to take, a new approach to apply. You are giving me new memories. My story has purpose, and all the seasons of the past have Your hand of faithfulness all over them! Beginning today, I walk in the fullness of who You have created me to be, and I own my journey for Your glory! Use me God, use my story, use all the pieces of pain from the past to bring hope to others. If there are any elements of my past, be it strongholds, generational patterns, or word curses, I break ties with those right now. I replace [list them out if you know them] with Your truth. I declare, You are doing a new thing, God. Thank You for loving me and for Your faithfulness.

Discussion Questions

1. What has been one of the toughest seasons of your life?

2. Where has the enemy tried to target you to believe lies about your identity because of that event?

3. What has been tucked down inside from a hurt that you have seen come out?

4. Thinking about strongholds, generational patterns, and word curses, what comes to mind?

5. Forgiveness is crucial to freedom. Is there anyone that you need to pray to forgive? If so, who?

6. What lie against your past do you need to break and replace?

8
The Battle Against Our Present

When God doesn't give us all the answers we want, we get to decide whether just having Him is going to be enough for us. — Bob Goff

Focus

The battle against our present began in the garden of Eden. Adam and Eve lived 24/7 in the presence of God. Psalms tells us that there is fullness of joy in the presence of God. Adam and Eve had everything they needed and were constantly in the presence of God. Satan twisted God's words and tempted Eve to step away from all she had, her best life with a lie.

If misdirection is the tactic of the present, then focus needs to be our antidote.

Focus: a center of activity, attraction, and attention; the state or quality of having or producing clear visual definition.

Here is where we must remember the promises God has spoken over us. Here we press on regardless of season or circumstances. Focus looks like placing boundaries in our lives to say no to some appealing things so we can say yes to godly things. Focus looks like pausing to ensure that our choices and actions today are supporting those promises that God has placed in our hearts. Eve got distracted. When we get distracted, it's easier to get lost in where we are going, what we are doing, or why we are doing it. We focus our hearts, minds, beliefs, and efforts here.

Declaration

This present season is the greatest determining factor of our futures. Regardless of the present season or circumstances, this is our life. If we don't establish a strong foundation in this season, we are likely to have to repeat aspects of it. It's normal to desire to rush through seasons or control them when we don't like them. Social media has done us a disservice, showcasing the highlight reels of everyone's lives. You know, those refining seasons, the healing ones, the lonely and dark places that we all have to work through at times? We all have them. Our seasons and challenges are different, but every woman struggles. Every woman encounters hardships, and equally, we all have the same opportunities to make the most of each season in our lives.

Consider it pure joy, my brothers and sisters, whenever you face trials of many kinds, because you know that the testing of your faith produces perseverance. Let perseverance finish its work so that you may be mature and complete, not lacking anything.—James 1:2-4 NIV

God doesn't give us trials to tease us or punish us. He allows trials in our lives to give us something to learn and grow from. If we read James 1:2-4 again with that lens, a trial or a tough season can be viewed that God is wanting to do more in us, and for us. Ask yourself this question, "What if God allowed me to walk _________ [name a season of life that was hard] to give me something?"

This is where the battle against our present lies, the fight to succumb to the now, fall victim to the narrative, and forfeit what is to come or celebrate what God is doing in the process.

Perspective Is Everything

When Chris was on his sixth tour overseas with the US Army, our fourth together, we knew it would be challenging but we had learned ways to communicate and support each other from previous deployment seasons. Every mission is unique. His role was a proactive approach to building systems and planning attack tactics against the enemy. The span of work was wide and the hours were long. Mentally and emotionally, he was tapped every day. The kids and I were living in Tucson, AZ and about to move to El Paso, TX. I was twelve-weeks pregnant. Movers had packed our house in April, Chris deployed in May, and it was now approaching August.

That season held more loneliness than I had anticipated. There was far less communication with my husband than what I desired, and if I'm honest, I wished several things were different. One night, tears flowed as I closed my eyes and prayed, "*God, my heart hurts, I need more from my husband, but I don't feel like he has the capacity to give more than what he is doing. God, You are my strength, You are my source of joy and my anchor. When I am weakest, You are strongest.*" I began to thank God for everything the season did have—His provision for each step of the move and deployment, the blessings surrounding me, my kids, my husband, and a beautiful temporary home to live in.

As my thoughts and words turned to gratitude, the tears decreased. I knew there was nothing more I could do in that moment, other than to keep praying and continue proclaiming gratitude. In faith, I knew I needed to trust that God was already at work. In surrender, I knew the only thing left was to rest in that truth. The following morning, I woke up to the sweetest email from my husband, thanking me for being understanding, patient, and loving.

Here's my point—we are going to encounter attacks, unexpected and unfortunate events, but these challenges are going to give us something, a gift that our enemy doesn't want us to obtain. Had I taken my desire for "more" to my husband at that moment, instead of God, I would have given power and energy where it didn't belong. I would have given into a rational distraction tactic from the enemy.

If I could sum up this battle against us in one word, it would be "misdirection", defined as the action or process of directing someone to the wrong place or in the wrong direction. Our enemy wants us to focus on what isn't happening instead of what God is doing.

Satan wants us to see:	**God calls us to see:**
Disappointment with plans	Expectancy for His plans
Confusion in communication	Clarity in communication
Closed doors as failures	Closed doors as provision
Withholdings as unworthy	Withholdings as protection for something better
Distraction as interesting	Relentless focus for His call on our lives
Division being celebrated	Unity pursued
Gaps of comparison	Gaps for refining
Hurts becoming identities	Hurts healed, used for His glory
Lies believed as truth	Lies taken captive, submitted to His Word

Seeking the Lord first in seasons of question and longing is always the best approach before acting. It may be a season where you are to fight, a season to rest, a season to wait, but He will speak. He will guide you. He is at work.

Seasons

Therefore do not be anxious about tomorrow, for tomorrow will be anxious for itself. Sufficient for the day is its own trouble.—Matthew 6:34 NIV

The term "seasons" has helped me to quantify and articulate what I was walking at various points in my life, knowing that just as summer always ends, and fall begins, so shall this too have an end. When I have rough points in life, I now associate them with a tactic of attack from the enemy. Different seasons and circumstances may bring forth different attacks, but the tactics don't change. Our enemy doesn't have new tricks—he operates in fear, in deception, and in lies. While the battles wage on, we fight, pressing onward to what He is calling us to in that season. We fight with a confident hope in victory that He truly is working all things together for our good. Sometimes the season calls us to fight in resting. Sometimes it's in action. Fighting should always begin with prayer and fasting to seek the Father's will in that season.

For everything there is a season, and a time for every matter under heaven:
a time to be born, and a time to die;
a time to plant, and a time to pluck up what is planted;
a time to kill, and a time to heal;
a time to break down, and a time to build up;
a time to weep, and a time to laugh;
a time to mourn, and a time to dance;
a time to cast away stones, and a time to gather stones together;
a time to embrace, and a time to refrain from embracing;
a time to seek, and a time to lose;
a time to keep, and a time to cast away;
a time to tear, and a time to sew;
a time to keep silence, and a time to speak;
A time to love, and a time to hate;
A time for war, and a time for peace.

What gain has the worker from his toil? I have seen the business that God has given to the children of man to be busy with. He has made everything beautiful in its time. Also, he has put eternity into a man's heart, yet so that he cannot find out what God has done from the beginning to the end. I perceived that there is nothing better for them than to be joyful and to do good as long as they live;
— Ecclesiastes 3:1-12 ESV

"Toil" is defined as labor, suffering. Are we to suffer through seasons? No, God has made everything beautiful in its time, and the very best thing that we, His daughters, can do is to be joyful and trust that He is at work in our lives.

Rewriting the Story

There are seasons that I would have given anything for a "redo." I was convinced that the next season would be better than the last, yet I never slowed down to heal from past wounds. Unfortunately, a few steps into something new, I found myself tired and defeated. I was going forward with a mentality of a "wounded past." I believed I was a "wounded person." When I realized that I had adopted that label as my truth, it impacted my belief. My tainted beliefs grew into other beliefs: worthless, unlovable, and undeserving. None of that was true for me. In fact, it couldn't have been farther from the truth.

And not only that, but we also rejoice in our afflictions, because we know that affliction produces endurance, endurance produces proven character, and proven character produces hope.—Romans 5:3-4 HCSB

It's easy to see the hurt and injustice. However, if we look at smaller details, we will probably notice a few other things that grew out of those tough seasons. For example, three days before my senior year of high school, my parents moved our family to Nashville. It was hard and I was angry.

The primary narrative looked like: "How could my parents do that? Didn't they know I needed stability? Look at what I went through. I can't believe they would uproot me like that."

A secondary lens looked like: "My parents must have had such turmoil regarding uprooting me my senior year of high school. They prayed so much for me, and truly did what they thought was best for me. "

Out of this challenging move grew

- One of the seasons that would prepare me best for military life
- Some of the most amazing lifelong friendships
- A job that paid for my college
- A job I loved in vocational ministry

- The church where I met my husband
- A healthy place to begin to heal from my past
- Incredible memories

The affliction of moving was hard, but the harvest it later produced is unfathomable. Nashville is where God saved my life. Nashville is where God redeemed my story. Nashville is and forever will be the place I now call "home." I almost missed it. If I had only kept my primary lens or allowed other people's limited lenses to shape mine as truth, I would have missed it.

We have a choice of how we look at our stories. **Our choices give authority and victory to either God or the enemy.** The more we rewrite our stories, focusing on what was produced rather than what was hurt, the better we get at seeing the purpose, value, and "fruit" of the tough seasons. The more we rewrite our narratives, hope abounds. The refining seasons equipped me to say, "I have gotten through that, and I will get through this too." Your value and truth may feel buried far below, but God is preparing you for a far greater destiny than anything you can imagine.

The Wilderness

When we despise our present season, our focus needs to be realigned on the Father. Hear me—you are not here by accident. This season is not meant to bury you, but to build you. You have not been forgotten or forsaken. You have not been left in the wilderness to wander with an absent God.

Consider it all joy, my brethren, when you encounter various trials, knowing that the testing of your faith produces endurance. And let endurance have its perfect result, so that you may be perfect and complete, lacking in nothing. But if any of you lacks wisdom, let him ask of God, who gives to all generously and without reproach, and it will be given to him. But he must ask in faith without any doubting, for the one who doubts is like the surf of the sea, driven and tossed by the wind.—John 1:2-6 NIV

If you are in a wilderness season, I want to encourage you to declare victory over the battle against your present season! God is inviting you to grow closer to Him, because, sister, there is more He wants to do in you and through you!

We are going to have to fight for the promise God has for us. The tension we experience are opportunities from the Lord to take new territory from the enemy. It's okay to not know the answer. It's okay to not be okay, but we can't stay here. We must trust and declare that the glory will rest with God. He wants us to trust Him with our every moment fully and confidently. God has given us authority; we can't allow ourselves to be misdirected. Our victory in Christ begins in this moment by the thoughts we think and the choices we make.

Our future of freedom and victory begins here. The things that hurt us and broke our hearts, made us overcomers. The things that left us empty and lonely gave us a foundation to build on. There are more narratives that built us as overcomers than we realize. Through the seasons and rewriting our narratives, we will begin to see the attributes of strength, determination, and resiliency through God that we already possess.

Steadfast

The hardest things in my present season are all things I have prayed for. Deployments? No. Pseudo-single parenting? No. But marriage? Absolutely! Kids? Yes! Community? Yes. Adventure? Yes. To grow, to be refined, to be used by God? All yes.

If God allows trials to give us something, then every season in our lives can teach us something. Our present season can prepare us for something more. We may not like it or understand it. It's human nature for us to long for more. But, when we complain and try to control the details, we begin to rob the blessing of what God is doing in this very season. I don't have the answers, and I don't like that. Sometimes, I like to ask, "what if?", and try to think about the opportunities that are present because of my circumstances. How can God use me here? What can I grow from this season? Who am I to connect with, pour into, or learn from now?

The steadfast of mind You will keep in perfect peace, because he trusts in You.
—Isaiah 26:3 NASB

Because he has focused his love on me, I will deliver him. I will protect him because he knows my name. When he calls out to me, I will answer him. I will be with him in his distress. I will deliver him, and I will honor him.—Psalm 91:14-15 ISV

To be steadfast means to be resolutely or dutifully firm and unwavering. A mind focused on God's Word and His character abounds in peace. In the Hebrew, the word for steadfast, *camak,* means supported by or to rest upon. What we rest our hope on matters. What we build upon either produces peace or panic.

Let's declare over our lives that God is at work. Proclaim that He is for you and not against you, that He has good plans for your life-plans filled with hope and a good future.

Come Lord Jesus, have Your way. I want an outpouring of whatever You have and whatever You want to do in my life!

Example Battle Strategy

1. **The Lie**—I need someone or something to be happy.

2. **The Truth**—If God has not given it, then there is still more for me to do, to learn, and to grow from this season. "*Let us not become weary in doing good, for at the proper time we will reap a harvest if we do not give up"* (Galatians 6:9 NIV).

3. **The Replacement**—I replace the lie that I need someone or something to be happy. I cling to Your truth, to make the most of this

day, and this season. In due time, You promise a harvest, an abundance. You care about the desires of my heart and I can trust You.

4. **The Declaration**—You have gifted me, and planted me in this place and this season for a purpose. Today, I release my excuses. I turn over my desires and surrender them to You. I release comparison, bitterness, and sadness, and replace them with joy and a confident hope found in You. Your Word does not return void, and You will not leave me here. I rebuke you, Satan. Get out, this season and my story belongs to the Lord. God, may the glory be all Yours!

1. **The Lie**—They have it together. So should I.

2. **The Truth**—God has designed everyone different. The same is true of callings on each of our lives. Comparison is the thief of joy. You haven't designed me to live her life or to own her story. You have created and called me to walk out mine. "*My grace is sufficient for you, for my power is made perfect in weakness"* (2 Corinthians 12:9 ESV).

3. **The Replacement**—I replace the lie with Your truth, that You are at work in my life. You care about the smallest details. You don't make mistakes. You have called me by name.

4. **The Declaration**—I claim authority over my mind. I take back my joy and celebrate who I am today. I celebrate what I have done and what more God is wanting to do in my life. Today the comparison stops. The shame ends here. I accept Your grace, God, and embrace Your love!

Declare it!

- God has not left me or forsaken me.
- I am chosen, loved, highly favored.

- God has a plan and a purpose for my life.
- I have been created for such a time as this.
- When I walk through hard seasons, I will not be consumed by the fire. The Lord will deliver me (Isaiah 43:2).

Practical Fighting Tip: Combinations

Combinations are multiple strikes or kicks to the attacker. Combinations are best thought about in three's. Punch, kick, punch. Elbow strike, punch, punch. Kick, punch, punch. The intent is always from a self-defense standpoint to allow you to get away safely and find help.

When we are being attacked in our present season, similar to a real fight, we do best to fight with combinations against the enemy. This looks like prayer, fasting, worship music, reading His Word, or connecting with a girlfriend to pray over you. The more we can stagger the plans of the enemy, the better our chance is for escape.

Prayer

God, I pray that You would help me see the enemy and the battle at work to rob me of my future. I pray that I would put a stake in the ground today and say, "No more, it ends here." Redeem the parts of my past that feel broken, heavy, disqualifying, or shame driven, and give me Your eyes so that I may see myself as beautiful and full of potential as You do. Cover me, Lord, as I stand firm in Your truth, fighting back the right enemy. You say I am, not the victim the enemy wants me to think I am. Expand my perspective that I may see the truth during lies, hope in the midst of darkness, and a path where there seems to be none. You are not only in every moment of my present season, but You have gone before me and Your plans for my life are for good, for a purpose, to prosper me, and not to harm me. Today I reclaim this season, and my story for God's glory! In Jesus' name, Amen.

Discussion Questions

1. How do you view your present season?

2. How do you need to fight for who God has called you to be?

3. What do you believe God is giving you in this present season?

4. What do you want this season to produce in your life?

5. What are three things you can begin doing differently to be victorious in the battle against your present season?

9
The Battle Against Our Future

"For I know the plans I have for you," declares the LORD, "plans to prosper you and not to harm you, plans to give you hope and a future."
— Jeremiah 29:11 NIV

One of the most shared, yet rarely admitted, struggles among women is fear. Am I enough? Can I do this? What will people think? What will happen to my kids? Does my husband love me? Am I doing enough? Do people like me? I feel all of these to my core. Seeing them on paper, maybe you see the trend that I do, all of these are rooted in fear, present or future based.

The months and weeks leading up to a deployment are truly one of the hardest elements of the deployment. Questions flood my mind, scenarios that lack any kind of answers or preparation. "What would happen if? What will this look like when? How will we…?" The present isn't the problem. In fact, Chris and I have had to check ourselves at various times because one or both of us have grieved what is to come. I have noticed that I really spiral when the thoughts get too much on the future rather than on what is here in the present. One particular day before he was to deploy in 2019, I caught myself filled with big emotions the entire day. I excused myself to the restroom, locked the door, and prayed,

"*God, I believe you have called us here and for this season. I trust You, but I am having a hard time. Give me strength for the moment, help me not to waste what I do have now. You have gone ahead of both of us. I trust and declare that Your plans are for good for my life. You are writing our story, and if this deployment is Your will, I want to glorify You in the process."*

I was afraid of all the unknowns. Whatever the future you are imagining or desiring in your mind, God wants to do exponentially more in you and through you. And His more? Whew! Bigger than we in our human limitations can comprehend. God invites us to trust Him. Think about it, we are pursued and desired by the Creator of Heaven and Earth. He wants relationship with us so that we trust His will and timing fully.

God has designed us uniquely in our mothers' wombs. He created us with purpose and intentionality. Why? To bring glory to Him, that the world would know about His Son, Jesus! He loves us beyond measure. Like the good, faithful Father He is, God desires to give His kids good gifts, when we are ready to receive them.

God Where Are You?

The word "doubt" comes to mind— doubt that the promises are for us, and we doubt our worth and capabilities for His uses. It's easy to have faith and confidence when all the things are falling into place, but when the waiting sets in, or the questions don't have answers, it gets hard. Abraham wrestled with this.

In Genesis 12 (NIV), God called Abram. God gave Abram instructions to leave his home and extended family, and travel to a new land. God proceeded to make him six promises:

1. "I will make you into a great nation."
2. "I will bless you."
3. "I will make your name great."
4. "I will bless those who bless you."
5. "Whoever curses you I will curse."
6. "All peoples on earth will be blessed through you."

Abram was obedient and left to follow the Lord. The Lord brought him to the land of Canaan. Others were inhabiting it at the time, so Abram moved on. Over the course of time, Abram traveled all throughout the entire land of Canaan. Before Abram ever inhabited the land, he built altars to the Lord all over it.

Throughout the next twenty to thirty years, God continued to tell Abram that He would bless him and make him a great nation. In Genesis 15:2 (HCSB), Abram inquired, "*what can You give me, since I am childless and the heir of my house is Eliezer of Damascus* [a slave]*?"* The Lord responded, "*This one will not be your heir, instead, one who comes from your own body will be your heir"* (Genesis 15:4 HCSB).

Both Abram and Sarai were in their eighties at this point. They took God's Word and worked to create it in their own power. Sarai gave Abram her slave, Hagar, thinking that was the only way for Abram to have a son. When Hagar became pregnant Sarai became bitter, and everything resulted in strife.

Don't miss this! If God has spoken something over us, or promised something to us, He will be certain to bring it to pass. We need to continue the path of trusting and pursuing Him while we are waiting on Him. This is a good word for us to rest in.

Almost twenty more years passed. Sarai, now named Sarah, gave birth to Isaac at the age of ninety-nine!

Can you imagine how many times Abram and Sarai, now Abraham and Sarah, fretted over leaving what was comfortable, wondering if they had heard God wrong? The faith it must have taken to continue believing they were going to be a great nation and that God would give them the desires of their hearts? Scripture doesn't tell us that, but I can only presume that they had deep seasons of doubt regarding the promises God had made for their future.

By faith Abraham obeyed when he was called to go out to a place that he was to receive as an inheritance. And he went out, not knowing where he was going. By faith he went to live in the land of promise, as in a foreign land, living in tents with Isaac and Jacob, heirs with him of the same promise. For he was looking forward to the city that has foundations, whose designer and builder is God. — Hebrews 11:8-10 ESV

God's Glory

Stepping out in faith is hard. It's challenging to navigate different places with new people, but it's equally challenging when those closest to us do not understand why we are making the choices we are. This is our life, and if we don't lead through it with submission and obedience, our dreams and hopes become reactive and fluid to people and circumstances—what we can see or create. Abraham and Sarah tried to create what God had for them. But here's the thing, God wants to do something so mighty in each of our stories that we are left to simply say, "It was all God, to Him be the glory!"

Growing up I identified with the label of a fighter. Not in the physical sense outside of martial arts, but with a deep sense of hard-headedness and determination to get what I set my mind to. I had come to a place where I had to decide if the story I desired for my life was what I was going to keep fighting for, or let God's story be elevated. We can't have it both ways. Trust me, I have tried. **We don't get to live by the world and live for God.** So I surrendered what I wanted and how I thought I wanted my story to play out, and I began to fight in prayer and lifestyle changes for who God was calling me to be. It was a hard choice to make, but there was no greater catalyst in my story than that choice of surrender.

There's no way that Abraham could have created all that God did, and the same is true for us. In the hand of our loving Father, our futures are limitless because we serve a limitless God. Our enemy would love nothing more than for us to continually apply circumstances and limitations to our lives that impact the decisions for our futures. **It's a dangerous thing when we begin to believe the lies of the enemy because they limit how big we can dream and who we can become.**

Dreams

God has always spoken to His people through dreams, and He still does today. In my late teenage years, I had a dream in which I was speaking to hundreds of women, encouraging them. I don't know what was said, I don't know where I was, but the picture was clear. At the time I think I laughed it off, simply looking at my circumstances, I couldn't fathom a path ahead to connect the dots. My life needed deep healing, and I was not even interested in walking with the Lord at that time.

If you have had a dream, or maybe God has audibly dropped something in your spirit, have you asked Him yet what it means? Have you asked Him what He would have you to do with it? I didn't, nor did I know to ask, but I wish someone had told me. It's not too late, sister. Those dreams are gifts from the Father, things our enemy would like us to dismiss or chalk up to a weird item we ate the night before. **Our confidence in His promises establishes the foundation for our path ahead.**

Maybe you have given up on dreams or laughed them off, or maybe the doubt of your value or self-worth is too great so that you don't even dream anymore. Go read Abraham's story again, God wastes nothing.

One of my favorite companies, Horacio Printing has an incredible resource to help women dream, plan, and pursue what God is calling them to with the leading question, *Who Do I Want to Become?* This resource comes fitted into all their annual planners or is available on their website. Here are the categories to dream in:

- Physically
- Relationally
- Professionally
- Financially
- Personally

Visit HoracioPrinting.com and head to their resources to grab a planner and learn more about tapping into your dreams. Before you begin, read this prayer with me:

Father, thank You that Your Word is alive. Thank You that You are the same yesterday, today, and forever, so what You have said once, You will bring to pass. I submit my dreams to

You and my plans to You. Forgive me where I have taken things into my own hands to control circumstances or timelines. I want Your way, in Your time. Renew my mind and heart today as I dream. Speak Lord, Your servant is listening!

Fighting for More

When the movie *War Room* released, I remember thinking, "This is amazing, but how do I figure out the Scriptures to pray for a battle plan? How do I develop a battle plan? Do I need a prayer room? Year after year, I waited for the resource that you are now holding. I felt the Lord nudge me, "Write it." I laughed. Two years passed. At the end of 2018, I decided, "Why not me?" I scheduled time to write weekly, listed out a plan to keep me accountable, and here we are. What started with continuous curiosity and desire now had a clear path ahead. It has not come without sacrifice. It has not come without spiritual warfare. But I believe that it has only affirmed that the enemy must hate what I am doing, and what I pray happens in you! Fighting for truth and freedom, and for who God has called us to be must terrify our enemy. The problem isn't necessarily today, rather the trajectory of the impact and influence our life can have surrendered to God's plan for us.

Trying new things, working new muscles causes discomfort, and don't we all enjoy being comfortable? Distractions pull us away from the important aspects that we desire most. Like Eve and Sarai, Satan offers counterfeits—things that look and feel close but aren't truly what that desire is. Human attempts leave us feeling limited because no human effort could ever fulfill a God-destined promise. If Satan can distract us away from the quiet with our Father, away from the work and the discipline, then we will not be able to confidently lock into the path that He has for us.

Billy Graham grew up in Charlotte, NC. He was uninterested in church and very turned off by his parents' invitation to attend a local eleven-week revival. Through the course of the eleven weeks, his interest peaked via a newspaper article regarding his school and the immoral activity transpiring.

A friend invited him to come hear the "fighting preacher." Skeptical, yet curious, fifteen-year-old Graham went with his friend. Intrigued, he returned the next night, and the night after that, and the night after that. The invitation came to receive Jesus, and Graham went forward… the rest is history.

Sister, we have no idea what God wants to do in our lives. We have no idea who is praying for us. We have no idea the potential that lies both within us and around us. The only way we will tap into God-sized dreams is when we walk in relentless pursuit and obedience to Him.

Billy Graham's journey is only one example, but it shows us why Satan works so heavily to cause us to doubt and get distracted from our futures. It also shows the ripple effects that we now see reflecting on his life and ministry.

Only Good Gifts

Society tells us that anything we desire should come quickly, and that anything that causes us pain, disapproval, or dissatisfaction should not be accepted. Pressing on, seeking the Lord, and getting on our faces in His presence are part of the training ground for spiritual victory. Anchoring to the Lord, rather than the world, will clarify and propel our deepest desires to what He has called us to.

God has planted those dreams and desires within us. He loves us so much that sometimes His answers don't align with ours. While we lack answers to understand, He knows full well that His answer will only guide us more into that desire at the right time. Why God didn't give Isaac to Abraham and Sarah earlier, we will never know. Why God had Joseph go through the time and discomfort as a prisoner and slave before being second-in-command, we don't know. Why did it take seven times to march around the walls of Jericho? The only answer I can think of is that God was building their faith, leading them through each step where their lives would be used as testimonies. By the time the promises were fulfilled, I wonder if these people were so deeply grounded in their relationship with God that He knew they were ready to hold all He had for them.

Don't be afraid of the tough stuff. Don't fear or fret the refining seasons, even if all you see right now are obstacles ahead. Start with new decisions and actions that invest in who God has called you to be and remain tied in daily and continuously to Him with confident hope. His Word never returns void. **He will never leave you desire more- only speechless at what He has done in you and through you.**

Behold

Behold, I am doing a new thing; now it springs forth, do you not perceive it? I will make a way in the wilderness and rivers in the desert. —
Isaiah 43:19 ESV

Have you ever looked up the word "behold"? I had not. According to the original Greek work, *ide*, the definition is simply, "see".

We see our mess. Our focus is on the valley or wilderness season that we are in. We see the obstacles. We lack the perspective and clarity to see the full picture and the path ahead. Sometimes we lack the energy to take one more step ahead. But God has gone before us, far beyond where we are. He is bigger than our feelings and our circumstances. He has given us all these promises, not only to trust Him, but to follow Him as He calls to us from our futures! He faithfully guides us every step through the valley, into the "more" that He has for us.

Behold sister, God is doing a new thing. It may feel like pruning. It may feel like going into a desert with the uncertainty of how we will eat or drink. Satan will want us to get trapped in what we see and feel. Like Eve, he will twist the very promises to have us doubt the faithfulness of God. Seek the Lord. Turn on worship music, get in the Word, sit quietly, and wait for Him. Behold, He is at work.

With God for you, and with over 3,500 promises speaking directly to your future, are there really limits that you are bound by? No—with God, all things are possible.

Example Battle Strategy

1. **The Lie**—Why would God use me?
2. **The Truth**—"*Being confident of this, that he who began a good work in you will carry it on to completion until the day of Christ Jesus*" (Philippians 1:6 NIV).
3. **The Replacement**—God made me and designed me with purpose! If He didn't want to use me, He wouldn't have knit me together so intentionally in my mother's womb.
4. **The Declaration**—Today, I take back my mind and my dreams and submit them to You, Lord! You have made me for a purpose, and in You I have both hope and victory. I rebuke the lies and distractions from the enemy and give my dreams to You! Have Your way, Lord! Your word never returns void

1. **The Lie**—If I do this, people will never understand or support me.
2. **The Truth**—"*For am I now seeking the favor of men, or of God? Or am I striving to please men? If I were still trying to please men, I would not be a bond-servant of Christ*" (Galatians 1:10 NASB).
3. **The Replacement**—Even if people never understand, if God has called me to it, then He will equip me, guide me, and bless me as I walk in obedience to Him.
4. **The Declaration**—Fear has no place here. In Jesus' name, I speak over my mind and my fears, and I pray that You cover them, Lord. I want to obey You and honor You above people. Help me to walk in submission to Your will and bring peace to the relationships that I care about most.

Practical Fighting Tip: Blocking

Taking hits are no fun and they still hurt, even with padding. Positioning our hands up by our face in a fist form, elbows tucked in will help protect us from hits, as well as enable us to quickly block. For example, an outward block is to guard against a punch or kick coming towards the face. When the attacker begins to move in, your front arm works like an ice cream scoop, making contact with your forearm and the attacker's body to deflect the attack.

Deception in our present works against the promise of our future. Blocking those attacks now, throwing our enemy off, creates a new level of space to either strike or leave the scene. Never stick around for a fight; there is nothing good for your safety, or your future there.

Prayer

Thank You for going ahead of me, but not leaving me where I am. You are faithful to always meet me, regardless of how many times I end up there, never judging or condemning me. Thank You for the dreams that You have planted deep in my heart and mind. The desires for the future that You have given. In Jesus' name, I rebuke the lies of the enemy. I speak against distraction and confusion and put on the full armor of God as I navigate the battle against who You are calling me to be. Your Word never returns void. I declare Your promises over my life—your plans are for good, not to harm me, but to give me hope and a future. Right now, in Jesus' name, I take both territory and authority back from the enemy over my future, my desires and dreams. I give this to You, God. Have Your way in my life, my mind, and my heart. Speak Lord; I am listening. Today begins a new path. Holy Spirit, help me to respond with courageous obedience. Thank You, Lord for how You have created me, and the desires you have placed within me. They are rich. They are wonderful and needed.

Discussion Questions

1. How would you have felt in Sarah's place, longing for a family, stability, and the blessing?

2. What has God spoken to you or showed you regarding what He has for you?

3. Is there a question regarding your future or a desire that you are afraid to ask Him? If so, what?

4. What lie does the enemy use to distract you from focusing on who God is calling you to become?

5. What are some dreams that the Lord has laid on your heart?

6. In five years, what do you want your life to look like? Why?

10
The Battle Against Our Calling

He has saved us and called us to a holy calling, not because of our works, but by His own purpose and by the grace He granted us in Christ Jesus before time began.—2 Timothy 1:9 BSB

God Chose David

The Lord has brought me back to the story of David recently. David was a shepherd. He didn't come from a home or any assuming circumstances that would have led to royalty one day. But God chose him. David was anointed by the prophet Samuel to be king. David received the anointing, then went back to tending sheep. Same clothes, same staff, same field, same old David.

Let's think about that transition for a moment by putting ourselves in David's place. We have just received this incredible word which will drastically change our lives, people witnessed it, then we are supposed to go back to chores and life as normal. I wonder if David had a few questions. I wonder if people ridiculed David as nothing externally changed. Scripture says he went back to tending his flock for fourteen years. This all matters because the pasture seasons are where we get refined and prepared.

Pasture Seasons

We are designed first and foremost to belong, and when we know why we were created both with clarity and purpose, peace and passion emerge for our calling. Pasture seasons can be anything that requires questions, waiting, refining, and obstacles. Pasture seasons are battle seasons. I find that in the beginning of these pastures and battles it is hardest to hear God and see what He is doing.

Our enemy does not want us to ever step into the very things that God has planned for us. But just like David, God has purpose in the pasture seasons of our lives, character building years that will impact generations to come. It can be frustrating to watch some people know and step into their gifts and strengths from an early age effortlessly, while some of us discover them post-pasture seasons, but each way has value. We are here, given gifts and our stories to spread the good news of who and what Jesus Christ did.

Who we are, even in pasture seasons, and the choices we make with our words and actions will have ripple effects in our lives, our children's lives, and generations to come. We all love the mountain top experiences, the success stories, yet we are most refined for His glory in our pasture seasons. It's encouraging; David was unqualified, he made mistakes, and his resume fell quite short in comparison to other kings, but none of that mattered to God.

As daughters of the King, we are called by name, royalty by relationship, and given purpose by pure existence.

No more living inferior to others
No more living in comparison to another woman
No more tearing others down to build ourselves up
No more bitterness
No more shame
No more regret
No more allowing the enemy to have access into our minds

Enough is enough. This is your life, and you only get one. This is your year. This is your season for breakthrough. From physical appearance or circumstance, David didn't look like what anyone thought a future king would, but God saw him. And God sees you. He sees your heart, and like David, you have been out to pasture during some seasons to train and grow. What will you do with what He has given you?

It's important that we accept the positive and negative experiences that built us and use them to create something beautiful. David was a shepherd; God is the good Shepherd. There was no one who understood the heart of a shepherd and the nature of sheep like David. Here the very thing that most might have thought would have disqualified David was the very thing people would share for generations to come—how he shepherded his flock, how he was anointed king and returned back to the pasture, and his heart for God.

Righteousness—Right Way of Living

The beautiful thing about God is that when He calls us to something, He will confirm what our spirits are feeling. When we were given the Holy Spirit, that is God's Spirit within us, nudging us along, speaking to us, and guiding us. The directive is usually internal first, but then God can use anything to affirm or confirm what His Spirit has been speaking to us.

The Bible has amazing verses providing guidelines of how we are to live and respond.

> *For the gifts and the calling of God are irrevocable.*
> — Romans 11:29 ESV

> *For consider your calling, brethren, that there were not many wise according to the flesh, not many mighty, not many noble;*
> — 1 Corinthians 1:26 NASB

> *Each person should remain in the situation they were in when God called them.*
> — 1 Corinthians 7:20 NIV

> *I pray that the eyes of your heart may be enlightened, so that you will know what is the hope of His calling, what are the riches of the glory of His inheritance in the saints.*
> — Ephesians 1:18 NASB

As a prisoner for the Lord, then, I urge you to live a life worthy of the calling you have received. — Ephesians 4:1 NIV

With this in mind, we constantly pray for you, that our God may make you worthy of his calling, and that by his power he may bring to fruition your every desire for goodness and your every deed prompted by faith. — 2 Thessalonians 1:11 NIV

He has saved us and called us to a holy calling, not because of our works, but by His own purpose and by the grace He granted us in Christ Jesus before time began.
— 2 Timothy 1:9 BSB

Righteousness means the right way of living. Righteousness is God's way of living. If we are seeking a relationship with Him, making ourselves available to Him, and actively working to apply what His Word instructs us to do, then we don't have to pursue our callings. God will guide us internally and externally to them. However, in my experience, it comes when I make intentional choices to pursue and live by His righteousness. It doesn't mean perfection, or even that my life gets cleaned up, it's a choice to align my mind, my heart, and my actions with the things that are pleasing, honoring, and submitted to His heart. Just like we have many dreams, we have also been called to many things. You can be called to be a teacher, mother, military spouse, stay at home mom, a nurse, a blogger, etc.

Righteousness—the right way of living with God provides guidelines and light to the current path. Whatever His answer or guidance for the season, His plans are for good and filled with purpose.

Purpose

In the military, there are roles and scopes of the job pertinent to the leadership level involved. Chris is a MEDEVAC pilot. He flies with another pilot, one medic, and one crew chief. The purpose of MEDEVAC is to respond to a call for help, fly into the battle, pick up the wounded, and get them to the nearest field hospital as quickly and safely as possible. Each soldier aboard the aircraft has full clarity of their role and the role of each crewmember. Without every soldier showing up to own and execute their responsibility, the mission would not be successful, not to mention the dangers of being in the middle of warfare, or the life of the wounded on board. Can you imagine someone pulling the medic aside right before taking off to tell them, "You aren't a medic, who are you fooling? You can't do this. Remember that last time you worked on a patient, and they died enroute?" It sounds absurd, but isn't that how our enemy tries to engage us?

Purpose has become this monumental thing that is solely about us individually. Society will tell us that our purpose is "you-centric"—Why am I here? What am I doing with my life? Why was I created? I believe this is one of the methods the enemy implements to attack our calling. If he can manipulate something to make us believe that we are more important, that our freedom matters more than another, or our dreams are elevated above what God has for us, then we should get angry and identify a person or system as our enemy. Classic misdirection.

But that's just it, we weren't created for us. We weren't given dreams and desires to only propel ourselves. From the beginning we were gifted and entrusted with things to help draw people closer to the heart of the Father, so they too can walk in freedom in relationship with their Creator. God being the good, faithful, and loving Father though, He desires to bless His children, and He only gives us good gifts. As we step into our purpose for others, we are blessed beyond belief with joy, clarity, and peace that we are fulfilling the very reason for which we were created.

As believers, we are called to be the church, the body of Christ, to love and care for people as Christ did. The greatest call we are given as believers is not to find our purpose, nor make our name great, but simply this:

*Go therefore and **make disciples** of all the nations, baptizing them in the name of the Father and the Son and the Holy Spirit.*—Matthew 28:19 NASB, emphasis added

How we go about responding to that call is where we find purpose, even in the battles of our pasture seasons. We see it in action when we apply the gifts and unique characteristics He has entrusted us with, working together to further His kingdom. Each season acts as a building block of preparation and trust. If we are responsible in our present season, like David, Moses, Joseph, Jacob, and Samuel, He will entrust us with more.

Contrary to what the enemy is trying to make you believe, you haven't missed it. You're in it. The seeds that you sow into your life today—your mindset, your attitude, your response towards others, and how you love people—sows into your purpose. The people you surround yourself with, sow into purpose. The way you navigate the battles and those pasture seasons, builds purpose. The way you show up and serve as part of the body of Christ, purpose. Let me encourage you—He has far more for us than we even know.

Made for More

For you were called to freedom, brethren; only do not turn your freedom into an opportunity for flesh, but through love serve one another.
— Galatians. 5:13 NASB

God chose you—to create you, to skillfully mold you, with love and intentionality—and He did it with great joy. He called you by name. Let that sink in for a second—the God of the universe; the One who separates the land from the sea, the light from the darkness; the One who created every plant, animal, and person still chose to create you. That tells me that without you, your story, your voice, and your presence, there would be a void. These past six battles are designed to keep us distracted, doubting, and disqualified. Plotted by the enemy, allowed by the Lord, these battles are tests to refine us and grow us ultimately into who and what God has for us. We get to choose if we will elevate God in the process or cower to the attacks of the enemy.

If I say, "Surely the darkness will overwhelm me,

And the light around me will be night,"
Even the darkness is not dark to You,
And the night is as bright as the day.
Darkness and light are alike to You.
For You formed my inward parts;
You wove me in my mother's womb.
I will give thanks to You, for I am fearfully and wonderfully made;
Wonderful are Your works,
And my soul knows it very well.
My frame was not hidden from You,
When I was made in secret,
And skillfully wrought in the depths of the earth;
Your eyes have seen my unformed substance;
And in Your book were all written
The days that were ordained for me,
When as yet there was not one of them.
How precious also are Your thoughts to me, O God!
How vast is the sum of them!
If I should count them, they would outnumber the sand.
When I awake, I am still with You.

— Psalm 139:11-18 NASB

I wonder if Satan is terrified that we will one day realize our power within God and the limitless potential of impact we could have on people who God has placed in our midst? What would it look like if we walked into this season of life, eyes wide open, fully awake with anticipation and expectation to love and serve others in our circles through our actions and words? What would change if we owned the circles of friends and seasons God has given us with His righteousness leading?

Purpose or Ministry?

Let's exchange the word "purpose" for the word "ministry"? It feels different, doesn't it? It puts a new focus on the intended effort for us as believers. Our own purpose or ministry is going to look different from anyone else's, and that is good. If God wanted us to copy another person, He would not have given us a unique DNA with unique strengths, because then what value would that have been? No. He saw a void. He knew that our stories, our journeys, our voices, our minds, our hearts, our skills, our talents, our strengths, our dreams, were going to be deeply needed with certain people in certain circumstances that would ultimately plant seeds and lead others to hope through a personal relationship with His Son, Jesus Christ.

This is one of the key reasons that Satan uses tactics of competition and comparison with women. **If our enemy can keep our focus in those two lanes, always striving, never measuring up, then he can keep us fixated on the wrong things, forever spinning.**

If you have ever thought your life and story were average or lacked purpose and meaning, you are not alone. Just as we have applied fighting tactics to other lies and battles, those thoughts are lies from the enemy. Think about where you are at in your life, the season you are in, the people that are in your life, the opportunities at hand, and the challenges present.

Allow the weight of this season, where you are, your area of influence and impact to set in. With no negativity and condemnation against yourself, I want you to close your eyes, pray, and think on these questions:

1. What has happened in your life that has deeply shaped you that you could help others with?

2. What are things that break your heart? What groups of people do you have a heart for?

3. What are gifts, passions, and strengths that the Lord has already given you, today?

4. What do you love learning about, doing, and sharing with others?

5. What are the kinds of stories that you want people to one day share about you?

Where our dreams, stories, and gifts intersect is where we find purpose and ministry. This is your call, this is your purpose. Lean in, embrace it. Even if you don't like what is coming up inside of you at this moment, allow the Holy Spirit to speak to you. This is where the enemy often wants to intersect us with thoughts of, "Oh man, I do not want that to be my calling! Now I am going to have to tell people about *that* season and I really wanted that to stay buried in the past." Rise up, friend; choose to proclaim life, freedom, and ownership over it. Where the enemy tried to bury you and disqualify you, that is the ground you were built on! **God didn't allow you to walk and fight through all that you did to waste it. He allowed it to shape you, to bring freedom in your calling to you so that you can now help bring it to others.** You were created for such a time as this.

Example Battle Strategy

1. **The Lie** — Because of my past, age, or stage, I am unable to do what I was supposed to.
2. **The Truth** — I have not missed my purpose or calling! God has plans for me, and they are good, filled with hope (Jeremiah. 29:11). What He has started in me, He will bring to completion (Philippians. 1:6).
3. **The Replacement** — God's timing is perfect, and His Word never returns void. He is at work, even now.
4. **The Declaration** — Today, I take back my authority over the calling on my life and the future ahead, declaring freedom and victory. God,

You have designed me with purpose, intentionally crafted me for the impact to make Your name known. Use me, God; I trust You, and I rejoice that You are working in the unseen. I proclaim victory over this season that is sowing into my calling, and I give You the glory in it. You waste nothing; use me as Your vessel, God. I trust in Your Word that there is a future ahead, it is good, and because of You, I have hope.

1. **The Lie** — I can't do it because of my circumstances.
2. **The Truth** — I may not be able to do something in a certain way, but I can still serve the Lord with my whole being, trusting God will use both me and my circumstances for His glory (Colossians 3:23-24).
3. **The Replacement** — I am not the victim. My circumstances may not be ideal, but this is my life. I have authority over it, and God is in this season and the next, faithfully leading.
4. **The Declaration** — Thank You, Lord, that You are reworking my vision to see my circumstances through Your lens. Through You, I am a victor. This season has been entrusted to me so that it might build me and glorify Your name. I don't understand it, but I will fight with joy, with hope, and with relentless pursuit of what You have for me in this season, in this circumstance. No longer does this limit me or disqualify me from what You have for me!

Practical Fighting Tip: Punching and Kicking

To effectively punch or kick, there are certain techniques to protect yourself and still make the right contact. The basic technique of a punch looks like holding your hand out in front of you, palm away. Tuck your four fingers, pointer to pinky into the palm of your hand, then fold over your thumb to protect and keep the other fingers tucked in. When you strike, you want to hit with the area between your knuckles and the bend in your fingers.

There are several types of kicks, but the most basic is a front kick. This begins with the proper stance, our fighting stance. Weight goes on the back foot. The front knee raises to waist level as toes are extended as high as possible. The ball of the foot becomes pronounced and that is the part we want to make contact with.

The details of the fingers and toes are minor, but these little details and seconds of preparation prevent breakage upon impact, creating the best chance of defense to get away from an attacker. These behaviors do not come naturally. Rather they are years of training, multiple times a week practicing the basic movements so that if ever needed, we are ready to respond instantly.

Our calling is within our journey. Daily choices, weekly practices in the small unseen things like our relationship with the Lord, our mind, and our attitude. In the process of training in the small things, we gain clarity in preparation to be ready when bigger things come.

Prayer

Thank You, Lord, that You waste nothing. You have purpose and hope that I can cling to in every season. Thank You that Your Word never returns void, so the things You have said will come to pass. You are doing a new thing, and I perceive it!

In Jesus' name, I rebuke the lies and distractions of the enemy to steal me away in the valley seasons. I replace the lies and distractions of what the world gives, things that satisfy for now but pull me away, with Your purpose and calling on my life. Impart vision and wisdom to me, God. I pray my mind and heart will be open to dream without condemnation, to pursue with great courage, and to take the next steps forward in obedience. My life is for You, and for Your glory!

Today, I pray for a newfound sense of clarity, purpose, and peace, knowing that You are leading every step. I pray that I will rest knowing that You have called me by name, wasting nothing of my story, but bringing it in Your time. In You, I am whole, lacking nothing. I claim Your truths as my victory banner, always ahead of me. In this moment, I declare a breakthrough from lies and what has been holding me back, and proclaim freedom over my calling, because You have said it to be so! Thank You for what You have ahead, and what you are working in the unseen. Speak Lord, your servant is listening. Empty me of me and fill me with more of You. Father, I praise you that Your plans are for good, Lord! This is all for your glory! Amen.

Discussion Questions

1. What lens do you find value in?

2. How do you measure significance?

3. What breaks your heart? What keeps you up at night?

4. What are dreams and passions that the Lord has placed inside of you?

5. Where is the Lord prompting you to realign?

Closing Thoughts

You have an amazing call on your life. Hearing your story, I can see the evidence of God's faithfulness and provision over your life leading you exactly to this very moment, for such a time as this. You see, where the enemy has deceived you to believe you are not worthy, unqualified, or incapable, these strategic lies that have been used against you to both distract and silence you. Right now, it's time to take back your authority in Jesus, and begin to live in the freedom that God gives! God allows seasons, tests, and trials so that we may be refined and glorify Him in the process. I caution you to be careful not to allow a season or a chapter in your story to become your whole story. What God does in you and through you, that is your story. How He provided for you, brought you into freedom, led you through every mountain and valley—that is the story.

Day in and day out, there will be attacks, distractions, and temptations. The difference between a woman walking in freedom and a woman who has a good life is whether her identity is in or out of alignment with the Father's heart. We are not called to simply have a good life. We are not even called to have a comfortable life. We are called to bring freedom to the captives, using our freedom in Christ to serve and love others. The truth is that when we give up our lives to be sold out for Jesus, allowing the fruits of the Spirit to pour out of us, something awakens inside of us. We trade the things we were deeply afraid of losing for things that awaken us, excite us, and echo joy to our greatest desires. There is nothing to lose, but your whole life to gain!

I want you to train with me, every single day. Read the word, pray, fast, take your relationship with the Lord to the next level, and identify the areas the enemy is targeting you and put a stop to them immediately! One step in the right direction is a victory. Immediate obedience in the natural yield's dividends in the spiritual, so lean into what He is asking and do it without delay. Ask Him to search your heart, and expose anything not of Him, then let it go. Lasting change happens when we humbly submit with a willing heart to be pruned and refined. Have hope in every season of your journey, not because it always looks or feels good, but because He is working. Even if the steps don't make sense to you or anyone else, know you can do this. He loves you beyond what you or I could ever understand, and He has incredible plans for you. Trust Him. Let's do this journey together. Let's discover the Father's heart for our lives, follow His Word through every battle, and bring that same freedom to every person in our circles!

You are a warrior, and I am grateful and humbled to be in this fight alongside you!

Appendices

Appendix 1- A Lifestyle of Freedom:

PRAYER

Prayer is a relationship. It's an exchange of listening and talking. What is even super special is that God speaks to all of us differently. There isn't a wrong way to pray, or a wrong time. There isn't a wrong way to hear from Him. The more you talk to God, just as you would a best friend, the more you become acquainted with His character, His attributes, His voice, and His heart. You simply cannot pray too much. In fact, Paul tells us in Ephesians 6:18 NASB, *"with all prayer and petition pray at all times in the Spirit."* Prayer is our greatest defense and strongest attack against the enemy, especially in battle. Begin talking to Him as you would your best friend. Whatever you are feeling, carrying, or struggling with, darkness cannot exist where there is light. There is no more powerful weapon we have than direct access to the Father. Pray.

When the attacks come, pray, and immediately replace those lies with truth. When the attacks come and we feel tempted to choose poorly, our breastplate of righteousness guides us in the right way to live, a new way to think, and a better way to respond. Start where you are with what you can. God knows you, knows your heart, and loves you beyond measure. Just as we rejoice when a child does something good, regardless of size, He does the same with us.

The Lord's Prayer

"This, then, is how you should pray:

"Our Father in heaven,

hallowed be your name,

your kingdom come,

your will be done,

on earth as it is in heaven.

Give us today our daily bread.

And forgive us our debts,

as we also have forgiven our debtors.

And lead us not into temptation,

but deliver us from the evil one."

For if you forgive other people when they sin against you, your heavenly Father will also forgive you. But if you do not forgive others their sins, your Father will not forgive your sins.

— Matthew 6:9-15 NIV

FASTING

One of the greatest methods of breakthrough and spiritual fighting is fasting. There are over seventy verses in the Bible related to fasting. It is never a method of celebration, but a tactic for breakthrough. Fasting is the concept of denying ourselves physical fulfillment in exchange for the spiritual outpouring of the supernatural. That means we are dying to ourselves; giving up what satisfies, what we have elevated, what we are chasing after; and surrendering it all to God to keep our attention, hearts, and efforts focused on what He wants to do. Fasts can be corporate, like Esther did, or private, like Jesus did in the wilderness. When we feel we are being targeted and attacked, or the Holy Spirit has prompted us that we are heavily elevating something to the point of reliance or obsession, it's time to fast and to be obedient to that leading immediately.

5 Things to Do When You Fast

1. Pray and ask the Lord, "From what would You have me to fast and for how long?"
2. Name your fast. (e.g., "Healing in my marriage" or "Freedom for my child")
3. Don't do what you normally do when that thought, or desire arises. Rather pray, worship, and seek the Lord.
4. Follow through. Even if the answer has come, or the waiting feels pointless, be diligent to be obedient to the timeline He has given.
5. If you lack clarity, do it anyway. Spiritual muscles are strengthened in obedience. Research, read, listen to messages on fasting. Stepping out in obedience and humility yields dividends in the spiritual.

Fasting isn't fun; no one likes it, but as believers we are called to do it. The Bible is very clear that there is a certain level of breakthrough and healing that only comes in the discipline and surrender of fasting.

Fasting will do more in doing less than you could ever do on your own. You are supernaturally provided for physically as you deny your flesh spiritually. Fasting opens spiritual doors that are impossible to open in the natural. — Landon Schott

SABBATH + TITHING

Tithing, sabbathing, and fasting are about us doing less in the natural so that He can do more in the spiritual. These disciplines yield a harvest over time because they all require faith and submission of things we both love and need. It doesn't make sense in our human minds when we are trying to do more, accomplish more, save more, or any category of more to give, to rest, or to resist what our flesh is desiring. These are fighting tactics, combinations that need to be in place regularly to position us in obedience and blessing. Look below!

Tithing

Honor the LORD with your possessions,
And with the first fruits of all your increase;
So your barns will be filled with plenty,
And your vats will overflow with new wine.
— (Proverbs 3:9-10)

Tithe means tenth. The tithe, the first 10 percent is what God requires of us. Obedience and honor lead to blessing. Look at the story of Cain and Abel,

> *Now Abel kept flocks, and Cain worked the soil. In the course of time Cain brought some of the fruits of the soil as an offering to the LORD. And Abel also brought an offering—fat portions from some of the firstborn of his flock. The LORD looked with favor on Abel and his offering, but on Cain and his offering he did not look with favor. So Cain was very angry, and his face was downcast. Then the LORD said to Cain, "Why are you angry? Why is your face downcast? If you do what is right, will you not be accepted? But if you do not do what is right, sin is crouching at your door; it desires to have you, but you must rule over it.*
> — Genesis 4:2-7 NIV

Cain gave a tithe to the Lord, but it was leftovers, a part of the crops from the ground. Abel took his tithe from the firstborn of his flock.

Everything we have is from God. By giving Him our best and honoring Him out of obedience with the first, the tithe, we position ourselves for supernatural blessing from the Father. When we are faithful with what we have been given, the Father will do more with the 90 percent leftover, than if we had robbed from Him and kept the 100 percent for ourselves. The enemy and even our culture will counteract this, because in the natural, it doesn't make sense.

Sabbath

Here's why sabbathing matters: resting and tithing positions us for humility and surrender. We aren't striving, creating, or hoarding out of our own strength. We are following the model from our heavenly Father to rest. In rest, we are reminded of dependency upon Him and positioned for blessing, knowing that God will do more in six days than we could have done on our own in seven. Rest can look like setting the boundary that maybe you don't check email that day, or you don't create anything new. Sabbath is one day a week, but like fasting, a day dedicated to the Lord to submit to His ways and His timing.

All these elements are additional spiritual tools that we must regularly apply to align us with the covering of the Father. When we are aligned with the Father's heart, we are positioned for provision, victory, and freedom. It may not look like what we imagined, or be in our timeline Think about it like this: We are not pursuing our heavenly Father, applying supernatural disciplines for an earthly answer or supply. We are petitioning Heaven, following the leading, obeying our Father's commands, going against how and what the world would tell us to do so that God will fulfill what His Word says.

"Bring the whole tithe into the storehouse, that there may be food in my house. Test me in this," says the LORD Almighty, "and see if I will not throw open the floodgates of heaven and pour out so much blessing that there will not be room enough to store it." — Malachi 3:10 NIV

Appendix 2- PRAYING BATTLE PLAN SCRIPTURES

1. Heart

As in water face reflects face, so the heart of man reflects the man.

— Proverbs 27:19 NASB

But the LORD said to Samuel, "Do not look at his appearance or at the height of his stature, because I have rejected him; for God sees not as man sees, for man looks at the outward appearance, but the LORD looks at the heart."

— 1 Samuel 16:7 NASB

Whoever believes in me, as the Scripture has said, "Out of his heart will flow rivers of living water." — John 7:38 ESV

Keep your heart with all vigilance, for from it flow the springs of life.

— Proverbs 4:23 ESV

Trust in the LORD with all your heart,

And do not lean on your own understanding.

In all your ways acknowledge Him,

And He will make your paths straight.

Do not be wise in your own eyes;

Fear the LORD and turn away from evil.

— Proverbs 3:5-7 NASB

And I will give them one heart, and a new spirit I will put within them. I will remove the heart of stone from their flesh and give them a heart of flesh.

— Ezekiel 11:19 ESV

2. Mind

You were taught, with regard to your former way of life, to put off your old self, which is being corrupted by its deceitful desires; to be made new in the attitude of your minds; and to put on the new self, created to be like God in true righteousness and holiness. — Ephesians 4:22-24 NIV

Jesus replied, "Truly I tell you, if you have faith and do not doubt, not only can you do what was done to the fig tree, but also you can say to this mountain, 'Go, throw yourself into the sea,' and it will be done. If you believe, you will receive whatever you ask for in prayer." — Matthew 21:21-22 NIV
Do not conform to the pattern of this world, but be transformed by the renewing of your mind. Then you will be able to test and approve what God's will is—his good, pleasing and perfect will. — Romans 12:2 NIV

Trust in the LORD with all your heart
and lean not on your own understanding;
in all your ways submit to him,
and he will make your paths straight.
— Proverbs 3:5-6 NIV

Set your minds on things above, not on earthly things. For you died, and your life is now hidden with Christ in God. When Christ, who is your[a] life, appears, then you also will appear with him in glory. Put to death, therefore, whatever belongs to your earthly nature: sexual immorality, impurity, lust, evil desires and greed, which is idolatry. Because of these, the wrath of God is coming. You used to walk in these ways, in the life you once lived. But now you must also rid yourselves of all such things as these: anger, rage, malice, slander, and filthy language from your lips. — Colossians 3:2-8 NIV

For the Spirit God gave us does not make us timid, but gives us power, love and self-discipline. So do not be ashamed of the testimony about our Lord or of me his prisoner. Rather, join with me in suffering for the gospel, by the power of God. — 2 Timothy 1:7-8 NIV

3. Words
Conduct yourselves with wisdom toward outsiders, making the most of the opportunity. Let your speech must always be with grace, as though seasoned with salt, so that you will know how you should respond to each person.
— Colossians 4:5-6 NASB

Let no corrupting talk come out of your mouths, but only such as is good for building up, as fits the occasion, that it may give grace to those who hear. And do not grieve the Holy Spirit of God, by whom you were sealed for the day of redemption. Let all bitterness and wrath and anger and clamor and slander be put away from you, along with all malice. Be kind to one another, tenderhearted, forgiving one another, as God in Christ forgave you.
— Ephesians 4:29-32 ESV

I tell you, on the day of judgment people will give account for every careless word they speak, for by your words you will be justified, and by your words you will be condemned. — Matthew 12:36-37 ESV

Set a guard, O LORD, over my mouth; keep watch over the door of my lips!
— Psalm 141:3 ESV

So shall my word be that goes out from my mouth; it shall not return to me empty, but it shall accomplish that which I purpose, and shall succeed in the thing for which I sent it. — Isaiah 55:11 ESV

4. Past

Not that I have already grasped it all or have already become perfect, but I press on if I may also take hold of that for which I was even taken hold of by Christ Jesus. Brothers and sisters, I do not regard myself as having taken hold of it yet; but one thing I do: forgetting what lies behind and reaching forward to what lies ahead, ***I*** *press on toward the goal for the prize of the upward call of God in Christ Jesus.* — Philippians 3:12-14 NASB

Forget the former things;
do not dwell on the past.
See, I am doing a new thing!
Now it springs up; do you not perceive it?
I am making a way in the wilderness
and streams in the wasteland.
— Isaiah 43:18-19 NIV

I have been crucified with Christ; and it is no longer I who live, but Christ lives in me; and the life which I now live in the flesh I live by faith in the Son of God, who loved me and gave Himself up for me. I do not nullify the grace of God, for if righteousness comes through the Law, then Christ died needlessly.
— Galatians 2:20- 22 NASB

Therefore if anyone is in Christ, this person is a new creation; the old things passed away; behold, new things have come. Now all these things are from God, who reconciled us to Himself through Christ and gave us the ministry of reconciliation, namely, that God was in Christ reconciling the world to Himself, not counting their wrongdoings against them, and He has committed to us the word of reconciliation. — 2 Corinthians 5:17-19 NASB

And He has said to me, "My grace is sufficient for you, for power is perfected in weakness." Most gladly, therefore, I will rather boast about my weaknesses, so that the power of Christ may dwell in me. Therefore I delight in weaknesses, in insults, in distresses, in persecutions, in difficulties, in behalf of Christ; for when I am weak, then I am strong." — 2 Corinthians 12:9-10 NASB

5. Present

And we know that for those who love God all things work together for good, for those who are called according to his purpose. — Romans 8:28 ESV

"For I know the plans I have for you," declares the LORD, "plans to prosper you and not to harm you, plans to give you hope and a future."
— Jeremiah 29:11 NIV

To humans belong the plans of the heart,
but from the LORD comes the proper answer of the tongue.
All a person's ways seem pure to them,
but motives are weighed by the LORD.
Commit to the LORD whatever you do,

and he will establish your plans.
The LORD works out everything to its proper end—
even the wicked for a day of disaster.
The LORD detests all the proud of heart.
Be sure of this: They will not go unpunished.
Through love and faithfulness sin is atoned for;
through the fear of the LORD evil is avoided.
When the LORD takes pleasure in anyone's way,
he causes their enemies to make peace with them.
Better a little with righteousness
than much gain with injustice.
In their hearts humans plan their course,
but the LORD establishes their steps.
— Proverbs 16:1-9 NIV

"For my thoughts are not your thoughts, neither are your ways my ways," declares the LORD. "As the heavens are higher than the earth, so are my ways higher than your ways and my thoughts than your thoughts."
— Isaiah 55:8-9 NIV

He cuts off every branch in me that bears no fruit, while every branch that does bear fruit he prunes so that it will be even more fruitful. You are already clean because of the word I have spoken to you. Remain in me, as I also remain in you. No branch can bear fruit by itself; it must remain in the vine. Neither can you bear fruit unless you remain in me. "I am the vine; you are the branches. If you remain in me and I in you, you will bear much fruit; apart from me you can do nothing." — John 15:2-5 NIV

6. Future

Being confident of this, that he who began a good work in you will carry it on to completion until the day of Christ Jesus — Philippians 1:6 NIV

"For I know the plans I have for you," declares the LORD, "plans to prosper you and not to harm you, plans to give you hope and a future."

— Jeremiah 29:11 NIV

For our light and momentary troubles are achieving for us an eternal glory that far outweighs them all. So we fix our eyes not on what is seen, but on what is unseen, since what is seen is temporary, but what is unseen is eternal.
— 2 Corinthians 4:17-18 NIV

The plans of the heart belong to man,
but the answer of the tongue is from the LORD.
All the ways of a man are pure in his own eyes,
but the LORD weighs the spirit.
Commit your work to the LORD,
and your plans will be established.
The LORD has made everything for its purpose,
even the wicked for the day of trouble.
— Proverbs 16:1-4 ESV

Now as to the periods and times, brothers and sisters, you have no need of anything to be written to you. For you yourselves know full well that the day of the Lord is coming just like a thief in the night. While they are saying, "Peace and safety!" then sudden destruction will come upon them like labor pains upon a pregnant woman, and they will not escape. But you, brothers and sisters, are not in darkness, so that the day would overtake you like a thief; ***for*** *you are all sons of light and sons of day. We are not of night nor of darkness;* **so** *then, let's not sleep as others do, but let's be alert and sober. For those who sleep, sleep at night, and those who are drunk, get drunk at night. But since we are of the day, let's be sober, having put on the breastplate of faith and love, and as a helmet, the hope of salvation. For God has not destined us for wrath, but for obtaining salvation through our Lord Jesus Christ, who died for us, so that whether we are awake or asleep, we will live together with Him. Therefore, encourage one another and build one another up, just as you also are doing.* — 1 Thessalonians 5:1-11 NASB

7. Calling

For I am already being poured out as a drink offering, and the time of my departure has come. I have fought the good fight, I have finished the course, I

have kept the faith; in the future there is reserved for me the crown of righteousness, which the Lord, the righteous Judge, will award to me on that day; and not only to me, but also to all who have loved His appearing.
— 2 Timothy 4:6-8 NASB

Therefore, my dear brothers and sisters, stand firm. Let nothing move you. Always give yourselves fully to the work of the Lord, because you know that your labor in the Lord is not in vain. — 1 Corinthians 15:58 NIV

Do not love the world or anything in the world. If anyone loves the world, love for the Father is not in them. For everything in the world—the lust of the flesh, the lust of the eyes, and the pride of life—comes not from the Father but from the world. The world and its desires pass away, but whoever does the will of God lives forever. — 1 John 2:15-17 NIV

We know love by this, that He laid down His life for us; and we ought to lay down our lives for the brothers and sisters. — 1 John 3:16 NASB

Notes

Chapter 2- The Woman and Warrior

1. R. David Freedman, "Woman, a Power Equal to a Man," Biblical Archaeology Review 9 [1983]: 56-58)

Chapter 3- The Armor of God

1. *A Spiritual Battle of Truth vs Lies | Devotional by Tony Evans*. (2018, September 11). [Video]. YouTube. https://www.youtube.com/watch?v=cqnWfvo7TgE
2. United Church of God. (n.d.). *The Belt of Truth - Armor of God > Free Bible Study Guides*. Bible Study Guides. Retrieved March 28, 2019, from http://www.freebiblestudyguides.org/bible-teachings/armor-of-god-belt-of-truth.htm
3. Oxford University Press (OUP). (n.d.). *ready*. Lexico.Com. Retrieved March 27, 2019, from https://www.lexico.com/en/definition/ready
4. Land, G. (2020, August 19). *3 Kinds of Ancient Roman Shields*. History Hit. https://www.historyhit.com/kinds-of-ancient-roman-shields/
5. *Faith - Easton's Bible Dictionary*. (n.d.). Blue Letter Bible. Retrieved June 20, 2020, from https://www.blueletterbible.org/search/dictionary/viewtopic.cfm?topic=ET0001302,IT0003351,NT0001783,TT0000191,VT0000987

Chapter 4- The Battle Against Our Heart

1. Brown, B. (2015). *Daring Greatly: How the Courage to Be Vulnerable Transforms the Way We Live, Love, Parent, and Lead* (Reprint ed.). Avery.

Chapter 5- The Battle Against Our Mind

1. Path of Love. (2014, June 4). *Dr. Caroline Leaf - Bring Toxic Thoughts into Captivity*. YouTube. https://www.youtube.com/watch?v=ZczIP_79jXs
2. Konnikova, M. (2017, June 20). *Why We Remember So Many Things Wrong*. The New Yorker. https://www.newyorker.com/science/maria-konnikova/idea-happened-memory-recollection
3. Leaf, C. (2015). *Switch On Your Brain: The Key to Peak Happiness, Thinking, and Health* (Reprint ed.). Baker Books.
4. Elevation Church. (2018, September 8). *Detoxing Your Mind: An Interview With Dr. Caroline Leaf*. YouTube. https://www.youtube.com/watch?v=Ea8pHeetkgo

Chapter 6- The Battle Against Our Words

1. *Musser, G., & Musser, G. (2011, September 15). Time on the Brain: How You Are Always Living In the Past, and Other Quirks of Perception. Scientific American Blog Network. https://blogs.scientificamerican.com/observations/time-on-the-brain-how-you-are-always-living-in-the-past-and-other-quirks-of-perception/*
2. *Yehuda Berg Quotes. (n.d.). BrainyQuote. Retrieved August 3, 2020, from https://www.brainyquote.com/quotes/yehuda_berg_536651*
3. *A quote by Frank Outlaw. (n.d.). Goodreads. Retrieved August 1, 2020, from https://www.goodreads.com/quotes/6507450-watch-your-thoughts-they-become-words-watch-your-words-they*

Chapter 7- The Battle Against Our Past

1. Oxford University Press (OUP). (n.d.-a). *forgive*. Lexico.Com. Retrieved June 21, 2020, from https://www.lexico.com/en/definition/forgive
2. *STRONGHOLD | Definition of STRONGHOLD by Oxford Dictionary on Lexico.com also meaning of STRONGHOLD*. (n.d.). Lexico Dictionaries | English. Retrieved June 21, 2020, from https://www.lexico.com/en/definition/stronghold
3. Freedom River Church

Chapter 8- The Battle Against Our Present

1. Goff, B. (2012). *Love Does: Discover a Secretly Incredible Life in an Ordinary World* (Later Printing Used ed.). Thomas Nelson Publishing.
2. *focus*. (n.d.). The Merriam-Webster.Com Dictionary. Retrieved July 8, 2020, from https://www.merriam-webster.com/dictionary/focus
3. *steadfast*. (n.d.). The Merriam-Webster.Com Dictionary. Retrieved September 9, 2020, from https://www.merriam-webster.com/dictionary/steadfast

Chapter 9- The Battle Against Our Future

1. *The Story of How God Called Billy Graham*. (n.d.). Billy Graham Evangelistic Association - UK. Retrieved July 28, 2020, from https://billygraham.org.uk/billy-grahams-story/
2. *Strong's Greek: 2396. ἴδε (ide) -- see! behold!* (n.d.). Bible Hub. Retrieved October 3, 2020, from https://biblehub.com/greek/2396.htm

Chapter 10- The Battle Against Our Calling

1. *Strong's Greek: 2821. κλῆσις (klésis) -- a calling*. (n.d.). Bible Hub. Retrieved October 11, 2020, from https://biblehub.com/greek/2821.htm

Appendices

1. Mercy Culture. (2021, January 3). *The Supernatural | Pastor Landon Schott*. YouTube. https://www.youtube.com/watch?v=9Mz9EfMuVuk&t=4489s
2. Mercy Culture. (2020, February 15). *Prayer & Fasting, pt 1: Undignified Faith | Pastor Landon Schott*. YouTube. https://www.youtube.com/watch?v=QFRD2Z08iDM&t=1580s
3. Listen to Dr. Tony Evans. (2019, February 28). *Dr. Tony Evans | Feb 28, 2019. Giving: The Generosity of Spiritual Growth*. YouTube. https://www.youtube.com/watch?v=7d1Oh-DEQ3Q

4. Mercy Culture. (2021b, March 28). *Supernatural Giving | Pastor Landon Schott*. YouTube. https://www.youtube.com/watch?v=UT7tcs-U3tM

Made in the USA
Middletown, DE
31 October 2021

50609176R10088